WHAT IS A JEW?

WHAT IS A JEW?

FOURTH EDITION

Rabbi Morris N. Kertzer
Foreword by Leo Rosten

COLLIER BOOKS
Macmillan Publishing Company
New York

COLLIER MACMILLAN PUBLISHERS
London

For Julia

Macmillan Publishing Company
866 Third Avenue, New York, N.Y. 10022
Collier Macmillan Canada, Inc.

A portion of this Collier Books edition is published by arrangement with Harry N. Abrams, Inc. (successor to The World Publishing Company).

Library of Congress Cataloging-in-Publication Data
Kertzer, Morris Norman, 1910–1983
   What is a Jew?
   Bibliography: p.
   1. Judaism. 2. Jews—Rites and ceremonies.
I. Title.
BM561.K45 1978   296   78-1999
ISBN 0-02-086350-0 pbk.

20 19 18 17 16 15 14 13 12 11

Macmillan books are available at special discounts for bulk purchases for sales promotions, premiums, fund-raising, or educational use. For details, contact:

> *Special Sales Director*
> *Macmillan Publishing Company*
> *866 Third Avenue*
> *New York, N.Y. 10022*

Printed in the United States of America

CONTENTS

Contents

Contents

Contents

Contents

Foreword

OF BOOKS there is a surfeit. Of books about Jews, there are—well, to put it mildly, a great many. What distinguishes Rabbi Kertzer's *What Is a Jew* is clarity, grace, good sense, and a rare serenity.

This is a wise survey of all those beliefs and customs, those ancient values and practices, those persisting traditions and inner commitments which, taken together, constitute what it is that lies at the heart of Judaism. (You would be surprised by the number of Jews who do not comprehend the majesty and the misery encompassed by those seven letters.)

And Rabbi Kertzer does all this without an iota of ambivalence. He cuts no corners and creates no bogey-men, evades no nettles. He strikes no poses. He hurls no anathemas. He gives us—Jew and non-Jew—patient, understanding answers to the most simple and complex questions.

So this is a most sensible and *humane* (because so keenly aware of the human) illumination of that much-discussed, oft-confused, forever tantalizing topic: "Jewishness."

Leo Rosten

Introduction to the Fourth Edition

A QUARTER of a century has passed since the publication of the first edition of *What Is a Jew?* The passage of time has eroded very little of the relevance of that initial presentation. Yet, historic events have brought substantial changes in Jewish life, and have, to some extent, modified some Jewish values.

In the first decade following the Holocaust, Jews had not yet begun to evaluate the impact of the death of six million of their coreligionists. Only as the effects of the trauma ebbed were they—and the world at large—able to draw lessons from the cataclysmic event.

Within the past generation, the State of Israel has grown from an uncertain infancy to a precarious maturity. In addition to its burdensome political problems—which lie beyond the periphery of this book—its more persistent concern remains that of its own identity. Will it become a secular national state, or will it somehow evolve into a community whose basic character will be fashioned by Jewish spiritual values?

In 1953, virtually no Jews had left the Soviet Union. In a new section for this edition, Part IX, I offer an evaluation of the dramatic changes within world Jewry that have taken place as a result of the latest Exodus.

During the past twenty-five years, the women's liberation

movement has reached a new crescendo of activity. Understandably, the Jewish community has not remained impervious to its influence and I have dealt with some of the new trends in the final chapter.

In my original introduction, I expressed my amazement about the extent of the world's curiosity about the infinitesimal segment of mankind who call themselves "Jews." Predictably, in the past two decades, smaller Jewish communities found use for this book. In its Portuguese translation, it is used in the public schools of Brazil for Jewish students enrolled in a kind of released-time program. The Norwegian translation serves a similar function in Denmark, Sweden and Norway.

On the other hand, the postwar Japanese eagerly sought out a translation to satisfy considerable curiosity about Judaism on the part of its intellectuals. Most puzzling to me was the recent translation of this book into Chinese. The Chinese people, one-fourth of the world's population, have had absolutely no contact with Jews or Judaism. Who among them sought out information about the nature of Judaism and the Jewish people?

One final note. Not infrequently, readers have challenged me, by letter and in public forums throughout the United States and Canada, commenting that this book answers every question but the one in the title. Some critics have correctly observed that my definition of a Jew is essentially an American one. Outside of the United States and Canada, a central religious authority(see Chapter 4) generally determines the status of a Jew on the basis of official documentation. In the United States and Canada, a simple verbal declaration is sufficient to provide admission to synagogue membership, the right to be married by a rabbi or to acquire a cemetery plot under Jewish religious auspices.

I must admit that I have no "last word" on the subject. Talmudic tradition imaginatively depicts a state of limbo where all of mankind's unanswered questions remain suspended until the dawn of the Messianic Age. Surely, the final word on *What Is a Jew?* belongs in that exalted category.

Introduction

A NUMBER of years ago, I invited a Japanese army officer, who was studying in the United States, to attend a religious service which I was conducting. At the end of the service, as we were walking home, he asked me, "What branch of Christianity does your church represent?"

"We are Jews," I answered, "members of the Jewish faith."

My Japanese friend was puzzled. He was a Shintoist, but he had read the Christian Bible. "But what are 'Jews?'"

"Do you remember the Israelites in the Bible—Abraham and Moses and Joshua?"

He recalled those stories.

"Well, we are those Israelites."

Major Nishi gasped in amazement. "What! Are those people still around?"

The majority of men and women in the English-speaking world are aware that the descendants of Moses are "still around." But there is, nevertheless, an amazing lack of knowledge about the Jews, their religion and their philosophy.

On the other hand, my experience has taught me that there is an ever-growing interest and a curiosity in these matters; so, though the beliefs and practices of Judaism are to many a closed book, it is a book that they are willing, even eager, to open.

Judaism is one of the oldest religions known to man, with a tradition that reaches back to the dawn of recorded history. It is a faith that has contributed richly to civilization and has grown and developed and kept pace with the changing spiritual needs of more than a hundred generations. It has a genealogy, a ritual, and a wealth of lore and custom richer, perhaps, than any other religion on earth. It has survived in the face of relentless persecutions, despite the fact that its adherents are vastly outnumbered and are scattered over the face of the entire globe.

For all these reasons, as well as for the special impetus lent by recent history, people are curious about the Jewish faith. This interest is shown, not only by non-Jews who want to know about the creed from which the concept of one God originated and out of which Christianity and Mohammedanism were born, but also by many Jews who, despite their ancestry, are personally far removed from the traditions and rituals of their fathers.

There are, of course, many learned volumes dealing with Jewish history, law, custom and belief. But most of these are, because of their very depth of scholarship, somewhat forbidding. The average man and woman has curiosity, but, usually, neither the time nor the inclination to delve into lengthy treatises. They turn, therefore, to the mass media: newspapers, magazines, radio, television, motion pictures. Both authors and readers realize that the answers found there only skim the surface of all there is to know about Judaism. But they help, nevertheless, to erase *some* of the misconceptions and to substitute *some* of the understanding so vital to human survival.

The questions included in this book are, of course, by no means exhaustive. No attempt is made to set down a manual of Jewish law or a system of religious practice. It is not meant to be a definitive formulation of what all Jews subscribe to, or what they should believe. I asked a number of friends, Christian and Jewish, to list for me those questions about Judaism which they most frequently encountered. I compared these with a list I drew out of my own experience with students in my college classroom. In addition, numerous queries came to me in the wake of an article appearing in *Reader's Digest* under the same title as this book. The hundred-odd questions in these pages appeared on all of those lists.

I have answered these questions with a minimum of theorizing and a stress on direct, factual information. I did so for two reasons: first, because it would take many thousand words for each question, rather than several hundred, to expound with justice on the deep underlying philosophy of the Jewish faith; and second, because I am convinced that there is a genuine need for this kind of brief introduction to Judaism among many who would not, at this point, read any more comprehensive dissertation.

It is my hope, of course, that some of my questions will whet the interest of those who read them—that my brief quotations from the *Talmud* will entice the reader to look for more of the same; that my few examples of biblical wisdom will remind him of the great storehouse of wisdom to be found in the Old Testament, and that my occasional quips of traditional Jewish humor will awaken a curiosity about the wealth of laughter that exists in Jewish lore. But, even if I fail to accomplish that much, I will still consider these labors worthwhile if I have made some Jewish readers feel closer to, and prouder of, their heritage, and some non-Jewish readers more understanding of Judaism as a way of life.

The questions are divided into nine parts. Actually, the division is quite arbitrary, for there is a great deal of overlapping and cross-referencing that help make most of the answers more meaningful. The part headings simply indicate the broad subjects which have seemed to arouse general interest: the basic beliefs of Judaism, the specific ritual requirements of an observant Jew—and their meanings, the traditions and customs, the relationships between Jew and non-Jews, the different Holy Days, and so on. Many of the questions might just as readily have been placed under several different headings, and the one selected represents no more than an arbitrary choice among them. It should also be pointed out that, though the answers are in terms of "what Jews do" and "what Jews believe," it is impossible to speak for *all* Jews on *any* subject. And, indeed, these very differences in custom, practice and belief are an integral part of the Jewish tradition.

I have deliberately refrained from weighting down the book with original Hebrew and Aramaic quotations. Since a very limited number of readers would understand them well enough to make their own translations, such references would only tend to obscure the thought and could have no real value. I agree, too, that something is usually lost in translation. Maurice Samuel crisply observed that a translation from the Yiddish is frequently not so much a rendition as it is a pogrom. To avoid that difficulty, I have usually preferred to paraphrase rather than to translate literally.

In general, this portrayal of the Jewish way of looking at things attempts to convey some of the warmth, the glow and the serenity of Judaism: the enchantment of fine books; the captivating color of Hasidism; the keen insights of the Babylonian rabbis into human relations; the sane, level-headed wisdom of the medieval philosophers; the mirthful spirit of scholars more than sixteen centuries ago; and the abiding sense of compassion that permeates our tradition. It is in this way—

and only in this way—that anyone can give a meaningful answer to the question: "What Is a Jew?"

I wish to record my thanks to several colleagues whom I consulted during the course of writing this book, particularly Rabbis Bernard J. Bamberger, Mordecai Waxman, Emanuel Rackman and Amram Prero. I am especially indebted to Dr. Moses Jung for many of his helpful suggestions. (The reader will understand that these scholars assume no responsibility for the material which the book contains.)

My grateful appreciation is extended to members of the staff of the American Jewish Committee Library of Information, headed by Mr. Harry J. Alderman; to Miss Naomi A. Grand, Mrs. Madeline C. Marina, Mr. Ralph Bass and Mr. Herman Horowitz for their valuable assistance.

To Mrs. Sonya Kaufer, whose editorial aid and guidance helped me to make this volume possible, I offer my heartfelt gratitude.

My special thanks go to Leo Rosten, who, in a real sense, provided the original inspiration for this book, particularly in the form and method of presentation.

Morris N. Kertzer

The Saga of the Jew

THE reader will recognize that in this book we will be seeing Judaism through a single dimension—that of the Jewish tradition. A second dimension is the history of the Jewish people, and a third, the literature which they have produced. For a thorough understanding of Judaism we really need all three. We need to know what happened to Jews through the centuries and to read the creative works of their writers. I will not presume to summarize the literature. But as background for some of the answers to be found in the following pages, I would like to touch on the highlights of Jewish history.

It is a story that begins, as does all history, in misty origins. The age of the patriarchs, Abraham, Isaac, Jacob and Joseph, and even the life of Moses, are the subject of much controversy among historians. Traditionalists accept every detail of the biblical narrative as fact. Modernists are inclined to accept only the broad outline of the Bible story as it relates to this early period. The settlement of the Hebrews in Canaan (later called Palestine, after the native Philistines) took place sometime between 1300 B.C.E. and 1200 B.C.E. The first kingdom, established under David and Solomon about ten centuries before the Christian Era, was a union of twelve separate tribes. After Solomon's death, Palestine was divided into two separate states:

Israel, comprising ten of the original tribes, and Judah, comprising the remaining two.

In 722 B.C.E. a disaster of major proportions occurred: Israel, the kingdom of the ten tribes, was destroyed by the imperial power of Assyria. That marked the end of *Hebrew* history and the beginning of *Jewish* history. The word, Jew, is simply an abbreviation of Judaean.

(It might be mentioned that the ten tribes were not lost: they were obliterated as a united people. But a number of well-meaning people cling to the idea that somehow the "lost ten tribes," like the sheep of little Bo Peep, will come home again. Several letters I received assured me that the tribes were still to be found in Africa, South America or the British Isles.)

At all events, Judah continued as a small nation leading a precarious existence in the shadow of mighty empires, until 586 B.C.E. when it was laid waste by the conquering armies of the Babylonians. Its capital, Jerusalem, was destroyed, and most of its residents were driven in exile to Babylonia.

These critical centuries, full of bloodshed and chaos, produced the greatest spirits of ancient Israel, the moral prophets —Isaiah, Jeremiah, Amos, Hosea and Micah. It was this group of spiritual leaders which gave the Jewish religion its distinctive character.

The second Jewish commonwealth, reestablished in 516 B.C.E., continued for six hundred years, through many storms and crises, first under Persian rule, then under the Greeks and Syrians, and finally under Roman domination, except for a century of independence under the Maccabees (see p. 161).

After the year 70 of the Christian Era, the Jews of Palestine were dispersed throughout the world—a few reaching far-off places in Central Asia, some settling in the hills of Ethiopia, and others in Italy and Spain. Although Egypt became, for a time, an important center of Jewish life, it was in Babylonia, that part of the world in which the first Hebrew, Abraham, was born, that a strong community was established, lasting well over a thousand years. Here, under benevolent skies, Judaism developed and created such historic institutions as the Synagogue, academies of higher learning, the *Talmud* and the foundations of modern Jewish law.

Jews came to Europe as early as the days of Julius Caesar, but there were only scattered settlements until the eleventh century. Then Spain became the center of Jewish life. In an era called "The Golden Age of Jewish History," under the benign rule of Moslems, Judaism produced more philosophy, poetry, science and religious literature than in any other period in its history.

The turning point was 1492—the expulsion of Jews from Spain after more than a century of relentless and devastating persecution at the hands of the Church.

Communities of some consequence grew up in Turkey, Holland and Germany, but it was in Eastern Europe that the concentration was most marked. Despite the hostility of Czarist regimes, a flourishing community came into being—largely self-contained—creating incomparable institutions of learning, a stable family life, and at least a minimum amount of economic security.

By the end of the nineteenth century, the Russian-Polish community contained most of the Jews of the world. Germany had a vigorous group, but it was relatively small in size. And the United States, which saw its first Jewish settlers in 1654, had barely a million Jews at the turn of the century (937,000 in 1897). Another one and a quarter million immigrated here in the first four decades of the twentieth century.

Then, in the 1930's and 1940's came the Nazi massacres, in

which almost forty per cent of the Jewish population of the world lost their lives. The deep trauma of that decade of horror spurred the drive for the re-establishment of Israel as a Jewish state, and as a haven for those who miraculously survived the holocaust.

Today, in all Europe there remains, except for Great Britain and France, only a skeleton Jewish community. For of those who lived through the Hitler era, only a minute handful have chosen to continue living among the haunting reminders of that period. The rest—all the rest who could physically manage the journey—have emigrated, either to the new and budding nation of Israel, or to the western hemisphere, where today the number of Jewish residents equals the total of Jews in other parts of the world.

In the United States, Canada and Latin America, a new Jewish communal life has been developing in the past several decades, based, for the first time in all the centuries of Jewish immigration to America, on native-born spiritual leadership and cultural resources. Since World War II, this new world community—and Israel—have inherited the torch of Jewish learning and tradition. For the great European libraries of Judaism have been razed; the shrines of Jewish scholarship in Poland, Lithuania, Germany and Hungary have been effaced; and most of the outstanding spiritual leaders of prewar Europe perished in the gas chambers and the crematoriums.

With the survivors, largely in Israel and the western world, then, rests the future of Judaism as a way of life. As in the past, it will be a way of life influenced and to a considerable extent altered, by the surrounding culture. But despite the changes and the innovations, the basic traditions of Judaism will remain and will be handed down to our children as cherished and intact as they have remained for these thousands of years.

[I]

WHAT IS A JEW?

God, where shall I find Thee,
Whose glory fills the universe?
Behold I find Thee
Wherever the mind is free to follow
* its own bent,*
Wherever words come out from the depth
* of truth,*
Wherever tireless striving stretches
* its arms towards perfection,*
Wherever men struggle for freedom
* and right,*
Wherever the scientist toils to unbare
* the secrets of nature,*
Wherever the poet strings pearls of
* beauty in lyric lines,*
Wherever glorious deeds are done.

PRAYER BOOK OF THE JEWISH
RECONSTRUCTIONIST FOUNDATION

What Is a Jew?

It is difficult to find a single definition of a Jew.

A Jew is one who accepts the faith of Judaism. That is the *religious* definition.

A Jew is one who, without formal religious affiliation, regards the teachings of Judaism—its ethics, its folkways, its literature—as his own. That is the *cultural* definition.

A Jew is one who considers himself a Jew or is so regarded by his community. That is the *"practical"* definition.

Professor Mordecai M. Kaplan, of the Jewish Theological Seminary, calls Judaism *"a civilization"* and describes the Jews as a cultural group, primarily religious, but not exclusively so, linked together by a common history, a common language of prayer, a vast literature, folkways, and, above all, a sense of common destiny. Dr. Kaplan refers to this group as *a people*, not in the national or racial sense—but in a feeling of oneness. Judaism is a way of life.

An important part of any valid definition must also include what a Jew is *not*. *The Jews are not a race.* Their history reveals countless additions to their numbers through marriage and conversion. There are dark Jews and blond, tall Jews and short, blue-eyed, brown-eyed and hazel-eyed Jews as well as those whose eyes are jet black. Though most Jews are of the white or Caucasian race, there are Negro Falasha Jews in Ethiopia,

3

Chinese Jews in Kai-Fung-Fu and a group of Indian Jews in Mexico whose origins are, to this day, a mystery to the anthropologists and the archaeologists.

Professor Jacob R. Marcus, in his book, *Early American Jewry*, reports: "A Quaker woman, about 1818, made a special trip to look at the first Jewish settler in Cincinnati. She turned him around and around and inspected him critically. 'Well, thou art no different to other people,' she finally said."

It would be equally misleading to speak of the Jews as a nation, though in antiquity they were. Today the Jews of Israel (together with their Moslem and Christian neighbors) are a nation. But there are no national ties that unite all Jews throughout the world (see p. 102).

The Jew is part and parcel of every community in which he lives. But he shares with Jews everywhere the distinctive tradition of Judaism and, to an historically unique degree, that "sense of a common destiny" to which Dr. Kaplan refers.

Those students of religion who take pleasure in cataloguing the dogma of the various creeds into neat, clearly defined categories, are inevitably frustrated by the Jewish faith. For Judaism, as the following pages will attempt to make clear, eludes a simple definition. It has almost no dogma and lacks entirely any formal catechism which all believing Jews—or even all Orthodox Jews—would accept. A number of years ago a Christian friend asked me what vows I had taken when I was ordained as a rabbi. The question surprised me—but my answer was even more startling to my friend. I had made no verbal commitments. I had not pronounced a single word of affirmation. I had made no declaration of faith!

To understand Judaism one must abandon the search for absolutes in ritual and in dogma and examine instead the broad *philosophy* which underlies our faith. Our rules of worship are far less exacting than our rules of conduct. What we believe about the Bible, about miracles, about a life after death, is secondary to what we believe about human potentialities and our responsibilities towards our fellow men. The changes we have made through the years in ritual and custom are of little consequence compared to the eternal values that have buttressed our faith through countless generations and kept Judaism alive in the face of every adversity.

Judaism has always been a *living* faith—constantly growing and changing as does everything that lives. We are a people whose roots have been replanted too often, whose associations with different cultures have been too intense, for our religious traditions and thinking to remain completely unchanged. In succession, Jews have been part of the civilizations of the Assyrians, the Babylonians, the Persians, the Greeks, the Romans and finally the Christian world. Ghetto walls were the exception of history rather than the rule. Inevitably these different experiences brought with them certain modifications and reinterpretations.

But even more marked was the inner growth—the deeper insight—that developed from within the Jewish community.

The most distinctive feature of the Jewish religion has been its hospitality to differences. In all of Jewish law will be found both an austere interpretation and a liberal one—and the rabbis have ruled that "both opinions are the word of the living God."

Our religion has had its dogmatists—those who thought it preferable to establish inflexible laws, who believed that religion should appeal to the heart rather than the mind, that human nature responded to conformity, and that symbols were more effective than abstract ideals. But we have also had our prophets in Israel, who demanded greater faith in man's potential, who refused to compromise in matters of justice, and who insisted that preoccupation with rituals and ceremonies was deadening to true religion.

Somehow the Jewish religion managed to develop without yielding entirely to dogmatist or prophet. The faith of the Jew demands that he fast on the Day of Atonement. But while fasting he reads the lesson of the prophets denouncing fasting unless it is accompanied by righteousness and kindliness. He comes to the synagogue to pray. And at worship he reads the words of Isaiah that prayer is useless unless it reflects a life of justice and mercy. Thus, Judaism has remained a flexible faith which sees value in symbols while it cautions against perfunctory ceremonial.

We believe in God—a personal God whose ways are utterly beyond our comprehension, but whose reality makes the differences between a world that has purpose and one that is meaningless.

We believe that man is made in God's image—that man's role in the universe is unique and that despite the failings that spring from our mortality, we are endowed with infinite potentialities for goodness and greatness.

These are our basic religious beliefs. The other questions touched upon in this chapter may be considered, in the words of Hillel, "only commentary."

What Are the Principal Tenets of Judaism?

JUDAISM holds that man can most genuinely worship God by imitating those qualities that are godly: as God is merciful, so we must be compassionate; as God is just, so we must deal justly with our neighbor; as God is slow to anger, so we must be tolerant in our judgment.

Some eighteen hundred years ago one of our sages taught: He who is beloved of his fellow men is beloved of God. To worship God is to love the works of His hands.

The *Talmud* speaks of three central principles in life: Torah —or learning; service of God; and the performance of good deeds, or charity.

The love of learning dominates our faith. As long ago as the first century of the Christian Era, Jews had a system of compulsory education. Education of the poor and the fatherless was the responsibility of the community as well as of parents! Nor were the ancient rabbis unmindful of the psychology of learning. On the first day at school, youngsters were fed honey cakes shaped in the letters of the alphabet, so that they would associate learning with sweetness!

The second basic teaching of our faith is service of God. From their earliest childhood, Jews are taught that He is to be worshiped out of love, and never out of fear.

The third tenet of Judaism is charity—the genuine charity that stems from the heart. There is no Hebrew word for charity other than just or righteous giving. Philanthropy, one noted Jewish scholar pointed out, is born out of two elements in our faith: the knowledge that all we possess is the Lord's; and the realization that man belongs to God.

Philanthropy, for the pious Jew, knows no racial or religious boundaries. According to the rabbis: "We are required to feed the poor of the Gentiles as well as our Jewish brethren . . ." No one is exempt from the practice of charity. The *Talmud* informs us that "*even one who is on relief must give to the poor!*"

True charity is anonymous and grows out of a genuine sense of compassion. And the highest form of charity, we believe, is helping man to help himself.

In Jewish tradition, kindness to animals is a purer act of goodness than helping one's neighbor. For it is done without any hope of receiving a return!

In the ancient academies it was common for the scholars to compete with one another in trying to devise the simplest formula for religion. The story is told of a Gentile who asked Hillel, the great rabbi and scholar of the first century, B.C.E., if he could tell him all there was to know about Judaism *while he stood on one foot!* Hillel replied: "Certainly! What is hateful to thee, do not unto thy neighbor. That is all there is in the *Torah*. All the rest is mere commentary. I suggest you study the commentary."

A century later, Rabbi Johanan asked five of his most distinguished pupils what they regarded as the highest goal in life. Each offered his pet formula. When all had been heard, Johanan said: "Rabbi Elazar's answer is still the best—*a good heart.*"

Another group of scholars searched for a single verse in the

Bible that would distill the essence of the Jewish faith. They found it in the words of the prophet, Micah: "What doth the Lord require of thee? Only to *act justly*, to *love mercy* and to *walk humbly* with thy God."

Do Jews Believe That Judaism Is the Only True Religion?

JEWS regard Judaism as the *only* religion *for Jews*. But we neither judge nor condemn the honest, devout worshiper of any faith. The *Talmud* tells us: "The righteous of *all* nations are worthy of immortality."

We believe in certain basic ethical concepts: decency, kindliness, justice and integrity. These we regard as eternal verities. But we claim no monopoly on these verities, for we recognize that every great religious faith has discovered them. That is what Rabbi Meir meant some eighteen centuries ago, when he said that a Gentile who follows the *Torah* is as good as our High Priest.

There are many mountain tops and all of them reach for the stars.

Do Jews Consider Themselves 'The Chosen People'?

THE words "chosen people" have been weighted down with many uncomfortable implications. Most of them stem from an unfamiliarity with the Jewish tradition and a misunderstanding of what Judaism considers its special role and responsibility.

Jews do not believe that they are endowed with any special traits, talents or capacities, or that they enjoy any special privileges in the eyes of God. The Bible refers to God's selection of Israel, not in terms of divine *preference*, but rather of divine summons. Israel was chosen to follow a life of great spiritual demands; to honor and perpetuate God's Laws and to transmit God's heritage.

Legend tells of the scene on Mount Sinai when the *Torah* was completed. God offered the sacred scroll to several other nations before he offered it to Israel. The Moabites felt that the Ten Commandments placed too many limitations upon them and turned the *Torah* down. The Ammonites, too, were unwilling to accept the restrictions upon their personal conduct. But Israel accepted the Law with no reservations.

Modern Judaism, therefore, looks upon itself as a *choosing*, rather than a *chosen*, people. We have accepted "the burden of the *Torah*," as it is called, and the responsibility for handing down its basic moral and spiritual truths.

But responsible Jews reject any degeneration of this sense of destiny into arrogant and hollow chauvinism or a confusion of responsibility with privilege.

One modern segment of Jewish thinking (the Reconstructionist group; see p. 121) has eliminated all reference to the "election of Israel" from its prayers. "There are so many other ways of developing self-respect," explains Dr. Mordecai M. Kaplan, leading spokesman for the school of thought, "ways that look to the future instead of the past, to personal accomplishment rather than to collective pride—that there is no need of inviting the undesirable consequences of belief in the superiority of one's people."

Even those who still preserve the idea of "the chosen people" agree that any suggestion of Jewish "superiority" denies the true essence of our faith.

Few Jews would disagree with Dr. Kaplan's assertion that "In a sense, every great people that has contributed to enlightenment and progress is chosen of God."

What Is the Jewish Concept of Sin?

A POSTSCRIPT to every Jew's life, uttered at his graveside, are the words: "For there liveth no man on earth who is so righteous that he sinneth not."

The Jewish concept of sin has grown and changed through the centuries. To the ancient Hebrews, sin was the violation of a taboo, an offense against God, for which a sin-offering had to be made. Gradually, over the years, this concept broadened.

Sin came to mean our inability to live up to our full potentialities—our failure to meet our duties and responsibilities as Jews and as God's people.

These "great expectations" born out of man's creation in God's image, are stressed in all Jewish teachings. A legend of the *Talmud* relates that when God gave the *Torah* to Moses, he called not only the Jews of Moses' day to witness, but the Jews of all future generations. Every Jew, the *Talmud* tells us, must regard himself as having personally accepted the Law and the high ideals laid down for his fathers at Sinai's foothills. Failure to live up to those high standards constitutes sin in Jewish life.

Jewish tradition differentiates between sins against mankind and sins against God. The first—a man's transgressions against his neighbors—can only be atoned by winning the forgiveness of the one who was wronged. Prayers cannot expiate such sins; neither can piety. God does not intervene to redeem man's duties to his fellow man.

Sins against God are committed by becoming alienated from our faith. These may be expiated by true penitence, which in the Hebrew is expressed as "return," that is, a return to God and a reconciliation with Him. This can be achieved only by an *honest searching* of our souls, a *candid admission* of our shortcomings and a *firm resolution* to bridge the gap between creed and deed (see Day of Atonement, p. 156).

Jews do not expect to pass their lives entirely without sin— for no man can be perfect. And there is a healthy caution, in Jewish tradition, against brooding over one's own sinfulness. "Be not evil in thine own esteem," the *Talmud* tells us in advice not too far removed from the teachings of modern psychology.

Do Jews Believe in Heaven and Hell?

THERE was a time when the idea of heaven and hell had some currency in Jewish theology. The Old Testament, though it has no direct reference to a concrete or physical world to come, does have some vague, poetic allusions to an afterlife. And during the period of Persian domination over Israel, some of the teachings of Zoroaster, among them the notion of a heaven or hell to come, became popular among the Jews.

But even then, heaven and hell were rarely phrased in physical terms. A soul delighting in a life well lived was in heaven; a soul tormented by remorse for misdeeds was in hell. Occasionally, there was some speculation as to the nature of Paradise—the reward stored up for the righteous. "May he dwell in the bright garden of Eden," was the common way to speak of one who had died. But there was almost no speculation as to the nature of hell. The form of punishment to be meted out to the wicked never exercised the Jewish imagination and there is no folklore dealing with the dimensions of an inferno or similar conjectures. Pain and anguish were too much a part of this life; there seemed little point to dwelling on the possibilities of everlasting torture. That is why such words as "damned" and "hell" have never been part of the speaking vocabulary of Hebrew or Yiddish.

Today, Jews believe in the immortality of the soul—an immortality whose nature is known only to God. But they no longer accept any literal concept of heaven or hell.

Jews have always been more concerned with this world than the next and have always concentrated their religious efforts toward building an ideal world for the living.

The twelfth-century philosopher Maimonides maintained that only the immature were motivated by hopes of reward and fear of punishment. The reward for virtuous living, he said, was the good life itself.

There is a parable often told about a visitor who came to Paradise and found it entirely populated by groups of old men, all bent over the study of the *Talmud*. Surprised, he questioned the heavenly guide, who told him: "You have the mistaken idea that the men are in heaven. Actually, heaven is in the men!"

Who Edited the Bible and How Was It Compiled?

No ONE really knows who wrote or edited the Bible. The men who preserved the Holy Scripture and gave it to the world in its present form were writers with a passion for anonymity. As a matter of fact, when the scholars were debating which books to include in the third and final section of the present Bible, anonymity was one of the tests they used. Except for the prophets, none of the authors were known. This modesty was not just a matter of individual temperament. Pride of authorship was alien to ancient Hebrew tradition. A writer who had something worthwhile to contribute preferred to attach his ideas to names already revered, such as David, Solomon or Isaiah. This explains why the Prophecies of Isaiah were not all the words of the prophet, nor all the Psalms of David and the Proverbs of Solomon the creation of those two monarchs.

The final "editing" of the Bible, like the original compilation of its wisdom, was also the product of group effort. Centuries of study and discussion on the part of our wisest scholars went into this task.

The Jewish Bible is made up of three distinct parts, which were edited (or canonized) at different times.

The Five Books of Moses, or the *Pentateuch* (the *Torah*), were edited earliest, in the years following 621 B.C.E.

The Prophets was organized in its final form about 200 B.C.E. This section contains the historical books, Joshua, Judges, Samuel and Kings; the major Prophets, Isaiah, Jeremiah and Ezekiel; and the twelve minor prophets, including Hosea, Amos, Jonah and Micah.

The so-called Holy Writings, which make up the third part of the Bible, was the most difficult for the scholars to agree about and took the longest period to compile. Many controversies raged as to which books to canonize and which to eliminate. There was no question about Psalms, Proverbs, Job and several other minor books. But a number of the rabbis questioned whether the Song of Songs, whose poetry obviously portrayed a very worldly love story, belonged in the Sacred Script. And others argued in favor of including the so-called apocryphal books, which were finally omitted from the Jewish Bible but later added to the Roman Catholic text.

When the last section of the Bible was finally concluded, it contained—and contains to this day—Psalms, Proverbs and Job; the five *megillot*, or scrolls; the Song of Songs, Ruth, Lamentations, Ecclesiastes and Esther (both read in the synagogue on special feasts or fasts); Daniel, Ezra and Nehemiah, and the two Books of Chronicles. Nothing that was written after the time of Ezra—that is, the fifth century B.C.E.—was made part of the Bible.

As far as is known, the first time that all twenty-four books of the Jewish Bible were mentioned as belonging together was about the year 90 of the Christian Era.

The sacred writings of Christianity were incorporated into works which the Christians called the New Testament as opposed to the twenty-four books which they called the Old Testament.

Those who have read both Jewish and Christian versions will note that the order of books is somewhat different in the Christian Old Testament than it is in the Jewish Bible. However, except for the additional books included in the Catholic editions, both texts are virtually the same.

Do Jews Believe Literally in the Miracles of the Bible?

OUR forefathers regarded the miracles of the Bible as literally true. They made no distinction between the natural and the supernatural, since the same all-powerful God who set the course of nature could alter it at will. The dividing Red Sea, the crumbling walls of Jericho, the sun's hesitation at Gideon's command were all accepted as *normal* historical events, no different from the fall of Jerusalem or the writing of the *Talmud*.

In the Bible itself, no reference is made to the *miraculous* nature of these happenings; in God's world all things are possible. History was not a matter for the *recorder* of events, but for the *interpreter* of events. So the descriptions of the Exodus from Egypt, Alexander's conquest of Jerusalem, the victory of Judah Maccabeus were entrusted to the religious teacher rather than the matter-of-fact historian.

Today, in the light of contemporary insights, many Jews look upon the miracles as inspiring allegory, rather than as actual historical events. This broader view is fully in keeping with Jewish religious tradition, which has always been most flexible. "The teachers and sages of a later period," Professor Kaplan tells us, "did not hesitate to read their own beliefs and aspirations into the writings of the teachers and sages of an earlier period."

A number of outstanding Jewish scholars, including Maimonides and Philo many centuries before him, have suggested that the authors of the Bible wrote deliberately in the language of the parable and the hyperbole and did not expect to be taken literally. Their purpose was to convey great moral truths in a way that would be understood and appreciated by the general public. The allegory served as an excellent method of teaching. And the Bible story has remained intact through a hundred generations.

A conservative interpreter of Judaism, Rabbi Morris Joseph, once wrote that though the Bible contains divine truth, the thoughts are expressed in the words of man, and are therefore imperfect. The situation is similar, he explained, to the rays of the sun which penetrate through a stained glass window. The light that comes through, not only loses some of its own brilliance, but takes on the various colors of the panes.

The biblical accounts of the miracles, he wisely suggested, should be read with the insight and intelligence with which God has endowed us.

Some people have devoted considerable energy to finding natural explanations for the miracles recounted in the Bible. The events that our ancestors considered miraculous were really, these people argue, an unusual combination of natural phenomena. The dividing of the Red Sea developed as a result of low tides and sudden high winds; the walls of Jericho tumbled because of an earthquake; and so on. Such explanations, while interesting, have always seemed to me quite superfluous. For those who insist on the "scientific" approach to the Bible must still find answers to explain why these "natural" phenomena all took place at such highly propitious moments. The eternal truths of the Bible, clothed frequently in phrases of poetic imagination, do not depend in the slightest on archaeological confirmation.

Do Jews Still Believe in 'An Eye for an Eye'?

FEW references in the Old Testament are as misused and misunderstood as the ancient Hebrew law of "an eye for an eye" or *lex talionis*. This is often pointed to as an example of the harsh code of the Israelites. Actually, however, it represents a great modification of the even harsher traditions practiced among the primitive peoples of the Near East before the Code of Moses.

The custom, in ancient times, was to hold the destruction of a vital member of the human body as a capital offense. A person who caused the loss of another's eye was put to death.

The Mosaic Code declared that a man must not suffer greater affliction than he had caused; hence "an eye for an eye; a tooth for a tooth," etc. And the Law of Moses went one step further: the courts were called upon to distinguish between accidents and deliberate acts—a distinct advance in the history of law.

As tribal life gave way to organized community living, the Jews of ancient Palestine decided that even this principle was too severe. The Mosaic law was then reinterpreted to mean the *cost* of an eye for the *cost* of an eye. The guilty person had to pay indemnity for the loss of a limb—much as he does today in accident cases. Any harsher punishments were strictly forbidden. There are many who believe that this is the interpretation originally intended for the biblical phrase "an eye for an eye."

Thus well before the New Testament was written, the Old Testament principle of *lex talionis* had ceased to exist.

Do Jews Still Believe in the Coming of the Messiah?

BELIEF in the coming of the Messiah—a descendant of the House of David who would redeem mankind and establish a Kingdom of God on earth—has been part of the Jewish tradition since the days of the prophet Isaiah.

As legend pictured him, the Messiah would be a human being

of very special gifts: strong leadership, great wisdom and deep integrity. These he would use to stimulate a social revolution that would usher in an era of perfect peace. But there was never any suggestion of divine power brought to bear. The Messiah was envisioned as a great leader, a moulder of men and society, but, for all that, a human being, not a God.

According to one tradition, the Messiah already has visited the world once, in the days of the First Temple. But his mission then was not crowned with success. For before the talents of the Messiah can be effective, men must be *ready* to establish a world of righteousness and human harmony. The second coming of the Messiah, it was held, was to be preceded by a generation of preparation. Before his arrival "his footsteps" would be heard, and men were to turn their hearts to God.

For generations the coming of the Messiah was a literal truth to every Jew. Solomon Maimon, noted philosopher of the eighteenth century, wrote in his *Autobiography* that when he was a boy he always slept under a heavy quilt, with the covers well over his head. But before falling asleep he always made certain that one ear was exposed, so that if the Messiah chose that night to come down his street, he would not miss the joyous footsteps.

Today, only the extreme Orthodox still cling to the literal belief in the coming of a Messiah. In the modern city of Jerusalem, many such believers gather in their synagogues to pray for a Redeemer to return to Zion.

Most Jews, however, have reinterpreted the age-old belief in a Messiah, not as an individual Redeemer, but as mankind collectively, who by their own acts can usher in a Kingdom of Heaven. When humanity has reached a level of true enlightenment, kindliness and justice, that will be the Day of the Messiah.

Do Jews Believe Literally in Satan?

THERE are a number of references to Satan in the Old Testament. But except for the brief period just before the Christian era, it is doubtful if Jews ever took these references literally.

In the Jewish tradition Satan was the mythical symbol of all the evil forces in the world. At times he was identified with the Tempter, the evil impulse which prompts man to heed the worst side of his nature. But even this notion was never too deep-rooted. For our religion teaches that God is the Creator of both good and evil and that His dominion, alone, is real.

In the Book of Job, the character of Satan was very real. He was an adversary who begrudged man's contentment and well-being and he was the indirect cause of Job's misery.

But the rabbis of the *Talmud* frankly debated whether the Book of Job was fact or fiction. A number of the most distinguished rabbis, noted for their brilliance and piety, contended that the entire Book of Job was actually a product of some ancestor's imagination—a parable or allegory similar to others to be found in the Bible.

The Persians, under whose domination the Jews lived for some centuries, believed that there were two great forces in the world, the God of Light and the God of Darkness. Under their influence, the Jews for a time sought to equate Satan with the God of Darkness and to blame him and other "fallen angels"

of the Old Testament for all suffering, calamity and wickedness. But gradually these ideas were rejected as alien to the
deeper Jewish tradition.

Thus, while references to Satan still remain in the Orthodox
and Conservative prayer books, they are generally considered
nothing more than figures of speech.

Is Judaism a Fatalistic Religion?

STUDENTS of religion have always been perplexed by the
question of whether our destinies, known to the mind of God,
are entirely beyond our control. From this stems a second question: if our future is already established by a divine Providence,
what difference does our will make?

Judaism, generally speaking, is not a fatalistic religion. Jewish teachings stress repeatedly that we are, to a large degree,
masters of our own destiny. Much of life is, of course, beyond
our control. We cannot choose the family into which we are
born, or our sex, race, color or native nationality. But the *quality*
of our life—our human relationships, our character and our
spiritual destiny—is, the rabbis teach us, our own to fashion.

Man is regarded as God's partner. God created a physical
world: the courses of the stars are already determined, the sea-
sons, the orderly growth of nature, all the laws of physics,
chemistry and biology. But man, if he wants to, can by his own
deeds create a heaven on earth.

Do Jews Believe That the Biblical Prophets Could Foretell the Future?

IN EVERY age there have been people who believed that some men could foretell the future. In ancient times, of course, this superstition was much more widespread. But in our own modern, sophisticated world there are still those who are attracted to the notion of trying to see beyond time. The cult of Nostradamus has had its counterpart throughout history.

But the great moral prophets, beginning with Elijah, were not regarded as soothsayers. They were looked upon as inspired teachers with great wisdom and insight rather than any miraculous ability to peer into the unknown. The Hebrew word for "prophet" does not suggest the powers of a soothsayer, but rather the courage of a man who *speaks out*. He predicts, not the inevitable, but the most likely consequences of wickedness and of violating God's laws. When Elijah foretold the tragic climax of Jezebel's life, he was simply affirming the principle that he who sows the wind shall reap the whirlwind. As a matter of fact, tradition ascribes greatness to Elijah not because of his gifts as a seer, but because he had the temerity to defy the most powerful and vindictive woman in Hebrew history.

Jeremiah's prophecies about the doom of Jerusalem always had a big "if" attached to them. *If* Judah followed a certain course, disaster would follow. There was no magic in his words—only the diagnostic gifts of a man who understood both the basic laws of morality and the complexities of international life. Jeremiah was the spiritual physician who knew the course which a moral disease would take.

Nothing in Jewish tradition would indicate that a human being, however wise and however inspired, living in a world dominated by Assyrians and Egyptians, would be able to predict events occurring when those colossal empires were faint memories, when the infant tribe of Remus and Romulus dominated the world, and the Temple of Solomon was destroyed.

Judaism wisely rejects this interpretation of the role of the prophets. Their immortality, to us, is based on their inspired insight—not on any supernatural foresight.

JEWS AND THE COMMUNITY

When the individual values the community as his own life and strives after its happiness as though it were his individual well-being, he finds satisfaction and no longer feels so keenly the bitterness of his individual existence, because he sees the end for which he lives and suffers.

AHAD HA'AM
(Asher Ginzberg)

Jews and the Community

THE core of Judaism is found in the Mosaic formula for treating our neighbor fairly, respecting his rights, his property and, above all, his person. One of the great rabbis of the *Talmud* declared that the world rests on three foundations—justice, truth and peace. Out of the first, said the rabbi, the other two emerge. If we deal justly with our fellow men, truth will triumph and peace will reign.

This passion for just human relations dominated the ethical teachings of Judaism down through the centuries. Every time a prophet saw an act of injustice he appealed to the conscience of the community. When King Ahab confiscated the vineyard of Naboth, the prophet Elijah issued a scathing denunciation of the heartless king and Queen Jezebel. Amos and Isaiah were equally excoriating in their denunciation of all kinds of exploitation. "Thou shalt favor no one in matters of justice," the law of Moses declared. And to the prophets the most unforgivable sin in God's eyes was to remain silent in the face of oppression, especially when it involved oppression of the underprivileged.

"If God doth not build a house," the Bible tells us, "in vain do the builders toil." An unjust society has within it the seeds of its own destruction. The rabbis of the *Talmud* used telling parables to illustrate this point. Why did the Tower of Babel crumble? Because the leaders of the project were more interested in the work than in the workers. When a brick fell to earth, they would pause to bewail its loss; when a worker fell they would urge the men to keep on building. The brick was more important than the man. So God destroyed the imposing edifice.

The law of acting fairly toward one's neighbor is the starting point for all Jewish teachings. Judaism has no elaborate philosophy of justice. Unlike that of Plato and Aristotle, Jewish teaching made little attempt to develop a systematic democratic philosophy. In point of fact, there is no Hebrew word for democracy, except that which is borrowed from the Greeks. But the social creed by which the Jews have lived for centuries is in democracy's highest traditions.

Basic to Judaism are these fundamental principles which are also basic to democracy: 1) God recognizes no distinction among men on the basis of creed, color or station in life; all men are equal in His sight. 2) Every man is his brother's keeper—we bear responsibility for our neighbor's failings as well as for his needs. 3) All men, being made in God's image, have infinite potentialities for goodness; therefore the job of society is to evoke the best that is in each man. 4) Freedom is to be prized above all things; the very first words of the Ten Commandments depict God as the Great Liberator.

The theme of freedom and equality runs constantly throughout the three thousand year history of the Jewish people. The frequent taste of injustice, as they wandered from country to country, reinforced a tradition already rooted in their faith. Thus, Jews responded readily to the thrilling challenge of the American Declaration of Independence and the Bill of Rights. And the French Revolution also found Jews sympathetic to the cries of Liberty, Fraternity and Equality.

It is no accident that the words, "Proclaim ye liberty throughout the land to all the inhabitants thereof," found on the American Liberty Bell, stem from the Old Testament. For love of liberty is woven into the fabric of Judaism.

The democratic ideal inherent in Judaism is naturally incompatible with totalitarianism of any kind—not only political totalitarianism, but coerced conformity of any kind. Dictators always found their Jewish citizens indigestible. Fascists and Communists alike have never tolerated the maintenance of the Jewish tradition because it represents a denial of the repression for which they stand.

The prophet Jeremiah exhorted his followers to seek the welfare of the country in which they live. And Jews have always felt the obligation to participate fully in the life of the community.

The voice of the synagogue will therefore be heard in all issues that would have aroused the ancient prophets of Israel: integrity in public office; just labor-management relations; civil rights and civil liberties; equality of economic opportunity; decent education, housing and health standards for all citizens; peace among the nations of the world.

One of the rabbis of the *Talmud* said: "If a man of learning participates in public affairs, he gives stability to the land. But if he sits at home and says to himself: 'What have the affairs of society to do with me? . . . Let my soul dwell in peace,' he brings about the destruction of the world."

Does Judaism Believe in Equality Between the Sexes?

NONE of the peoples of antiquity practiced equality between the sexes as we know it today. In a few unique matriarchal societies, women held the ruling position while men played the distinctly secondary, less exalted role. But in the overwhelming majority of ancient civilizations, including the Jewish world, these positions were quite reversed. With only a few exceptions, men were the political, social and religious leaders. They enjoyed numerous legal and religious rights denied to women and a distinctly superior social status.

Despite this inequality, however, the position of women in ancient Israel was considerably above that of their sisters in other parts of the world.

For one thing, biblical law concerning marital fidelity makes no distinction between husband and wife. There were no double standards of chastity among Jews, as were common in the rest of the Middle East. The frequent biblical references to love and friendship in the marriages of the elders of Israel are a far cry from the chattel relationship between man and wife among the rest of the desert peoples, and even, in most instances, among the Greeks and Romans as well.

Outstanding qualities of leadership and wisdom were sometimes acknowledged among Jewish women of antiquity. The judgment of Deborah was greatly valued; Miriam, sister of Moses, stood high in the ranks of the leaders. And the *Talmud* also recounts with admiration, the wisdom and scholarship of several unusual women, such as Beruriah, wife of Rabbi Meir, whose insights into Jewish law sometimes outshone those of her famous husband.

Some Jewish women achieved fame as lecturers in medieval Europe in an age when the general community treated women as little better than serfs. Dulcie, the daughter of the distinguished Rabbi Eleazer of Worms, in addition to supporting her family, was noted for her brilliant Sabbath discourses on Jewish law. Several other women of the fifteenth century were equally noted for their gifts as teachers and interpreters of the Law.

Furthermore, as wives and mothers Jewish women have always enjoyed a position of such reverence and esteem as to make them frequent powers behind the throne (see p. 67).

The rabbis tell of a pious couple who, because they had no children, decided to go their separate ways. Each remarried— and both selected wicked mates. In the end, the pious man was corrupted by his evil wife; the wicked man was redeemed by his pious spouse. The moral of the story, said the rabbis, is that "It all depends on the wife."

It must be pointed out that women were so fully occupied with their domestic duties, that it was impossible for them to become involved in the social and religious affairs of the community. Jewish law provides, for example, that women are excused from any rituals that must be performed at a specific time, since their responsibilities to crying or hungry children and other family needs take priority.

In the western world, the social and communal role of Jewish women slowly rose to greater and greater equality, along with that of their non-Jewish neighbors. In religious affairs, however, changes have been slower. Today, in orthodox practice, women are still not permitted to institute divorce proceedings or make up a part of the *minyan*, or quorum of ten Jews required for all religious ritual. In liberal circles, women are now ordained as rabbis and the number is likely to increase; both Reform and Conservative synagogues have abolished the separation of men and women into different pews; and in Reform ceremonies there is no insistence on a male quorum for worship.

Do Jews Have Parochial Schools?

IN THE early 1970's there were more than half a million children receiving Jewish education. Approximately seventy-five thousand were enrolled in private all-day schools. They are not parochial schools in the usual sense: they are not attached to parishes or synagogues. Unlike Roman Catholic or Lutheran church schools, the Jewish all-day schools are not under the control of a rabbinical body. The school boards are composed of laymen as well as rabbis; the schools are financed largely by tuition fees and private contributions; and the teachers of general subjects are, with few exceptions, secular.

The curriculum of the Jewish all-day schools parallels that of the public schools for half a day; the remaining hours are devoted to religious studies.

American Jews are sharply divided on the issue of all-day schools. Supporters see in them a reflection of the traditional

American hospitality to differences, which permits each religious group to combine the teachings of its faith with secular studies, so long as children are taught fellowship and kinship with all Americans. Those who oppose the all-day schools are concerned about weakening the fibre of the public school system by separating children on the basis of religion and see also a danger of developing social barriers between children, since the school is a proving ground for many lasting friendships.

Although all-day Jewish education is an established entity in American Jewish life, the vast majority of parents continue to send their children to the public schools.

What Is the Jewish Attitude Toward Manual Labor?

TRADITIONALLY, Judaism has always regarded labor as sacred. The tilling of the soil; the fashioning of tools; the work of the carpenter, the shoe maker and the blacksmith were all looked upon as reflections of the dignity of man.

Respect for manual labor is also often stressed in the *Talmud*. A second-century rabbi reminds us that the commandment about observing the Sabbath begins with the admonition: "Six days shalt thou labor . . ." A talmudic proverb declares, "He who does not teach his son a trade, teaches him thievery." And in the many parables of the *Talmud*, God, the Creator, is portrayed as a worker, a builder and an architect.

Many of ancient Judaism's most revered rabbis earned their livelihood as woodchoppers, blacksmiths or carpenters. The men who are credited with writing the *Talmud* and with authoring most of ancient Jewish law were not paid for these learned tasks. As a matter of fact, Jewish law forbade anyone to earn a living through religion. "Do not make the *Torah* a spade to dig with," is the way this injunction reads.

For many centuries—almost until modern times—rabbis were not allowed to receive any compensation for their duties. Even when these duties became full-time occupations, the formula that was adopted did not provide payment for learning or teaching, but rather *for the time taken from earning a livelihood.*

The traditional Jewish appreciation of the dignity of labor contrasts with that of other ancient peoples. The word, "school," for example, stems from the Greek word for leisure. For in the Hellenic tradition only the wealthy, or leisure, classes could become enlightened. Judaism, on the other hand, maintains that each human being must share the burden of producing mankind's needs. Thus, the Greek word for leisure has no counterpart in the Hebrew; the ancient Jews called it idleness, and considered it the breeding ground for much human mischief.

For a span of several centuries, however, when Jews were confined to the ghettoes of medieval Europe, the traditional Jewish attitude toward physical labor changed. During that period Jews were forbidden to own land and to work at a great many different tasks. They were forced to live in large cities where they could only manage to overcome the restrictions imposed on them by engaging in business or the professions. As a result, Jews began to view manual labor as somewhat degrading.

But with the destruction of the ghetto came a return to the deeper tradition. Jewish writers and philosophers called ringingly for a return to the soil and a renewed respect for the work of our hands. The development of the Zionist movement with its zealous drive for a Jewish resettlement of Palestine, was based not only on the physical return of Israel to the land of our Fathers, but also on the redevelopment of the biblical promised land through our own laborious efforts.

Today the dignity of labor is a cornerstone of life in modern Israel and among Jews of every land.

Is Reverence for the Aged Basic to Judaism?

I ONCE asked a Chinese philosopher how it was that Judaism and Confucianism had so much in common—respect for learning, emphasis on the family virtues and reverence for the aged. He answered in a matter-of-fact way: "We're both very old civilizations, the Chinese and the Jews. After so many millennia of human experience, one is bound to gain penetrating insights into the human heart."

Out of our millennia of human experience, then, stems the realization that the mellow wisdom of old age is precious. In Hebrew the words, "old man," are almost synonymous with "wise man." "He who learns from the old is like one who eats ripe grapes and drinks old wine," says the *Talmud*, and, "The older scholars grow, the greater their wisdom."

Judaism has always placed a premium on the experience which comes with years. Youth, it was recognized, had the advantage of profiting from the experience of its elders, but the young were cautioned not to boast about their broader horizons: "We are pygmies on the shoulders of giants."

Reverence for the aged was also translated into practical provisions for their care. As long ago as the Middle Ages, when in other cultures old age brought lonely, barren and often hungry years, the Jewish community built homes for its elderly members—not to remove them from their family circle, but to provide happier, more congenial surroundings among people of their own generation. It was a *mitzvah*, a religious duty, to give the aged every comfort in life.

Courtesy to the elderly was part of the fabric of Jewish living. One always stood in the presence of the aged. A parent's seat at the dining table was never used in his absence. One did not contradict an older person, even if what he said was incorrect.

As a youngster, I studied in the home of a learned rabbi, a well-known scholar in our community. He was a man in his early fifties and had a fine grey-black beard. The rabbi's father, who lived in the same home, was in his eighties. His beard was a patriarchal snow-white. I still recall vividly a time when the father stalked into his son's study and, despite the presence of several pupils, began to berate the rabbi unmercifully: "Jacob, you are spending too much time on worldly affairs . . . too little time on studying! If you don't change your way of life, you'll grow into an ignoramus!" The mere thought that 'our Rabbi' could ever be called an ignoramus shocked us. But the son answered simply: "Yes, father, I'll try to do better." "Thou shalt rise up before the hoary head, and honor the face of the old man," says the Bible.

In the summer of 1952, in the State of Israel, I saw this traditional reverence for the aged translated into modern terms. In a brand-new village called Holon, built by Israeli workers, I saw a beautiful area of "garden apartments" created especially for the elderly parents of the hard-working Israelis. Out of the desolate sand dunes of the Mediterranean shore, this pioneer community had built an idyllic haven for the comfort of the aging, full of grace and charm and without the faintest suggestion of institutional living. Each old couple had their own apartment, with neat flower beds and attractive lawns on all sides. The sunset years, it was clear, would be a time of beauty in a world of fragrant flowers, fine music and the sweet companionship of happy friends.

Do Jews Favor Capital Punishment?

THE Jewish attitude toward capital punishment presents a graphic example of how the Jewish tradition has evolved and changed over the centuries.

The commandment of the Bible declares: "He who takes a life shall be put to death." But very early in Jewish history, there developed among the social and religious leaders of the people a revulsion against legal execution. The literal interpretation of the biblical injunction was hedged with one safeguard after another to insure the accused against miscarriage of justice. Those safeguards finally became so involved that capital punishment virtually ceased to exist.

Theoretically, according to the *Talmud*, the twenty-three-man court established to judge murder cases had the right to pass a sentence of death on the guilty prisoner. But before they could do so, the prosecutor had to prove that the crime was deliberate and premeditated. This could only be done by producing two witnesses who had actually heard the defendant declare that he was about to commit the crime. In addition, the two witnesses also had to testify that they had quoted chapter and verse from the Book of Exodus to him to warn him of the gravity of his intentions. Circumstantial evidence, the basis of most trials, was unacceptable.

Furthermore, if these virtually impossible conditions were met, and the twenty-three judges voted *unanimously* for the death sentence, the *Talmud* ruled that the defendant must be acquitted! The rabbis reasoned that if not one of the twenty-three could find some extenuating circumstance, the atmosphere of the trial must have been charged with prejudice!

All of these subtleties had just one goal—to leave the biblical law unchanged in letter but modified completely in spirit. For the verdict of death was irretrievable. And the creators of Jewish law trembled before the possibility of tampering wrongly with the will of the Creator of life.

In modern Israel, capital punishment, since 1954, has been forbidden by law except in cases of genocide, acts of terror during war, and grave security violations during wartime, such as the use of high explosives. Even so, the death penalty is not mandatory and has been invoked only once, in the case of the mass murderer, Adolf Eichmann.

The Jewish tradition which stresses the sanctity of life is reflected in the report of Tirat Zvi, a religious settlement in modern Galilee, whose young residents fasted for several days because they had been compelled to kill some Arabs who had attacked their community. The deeply ingrained value placed on all human life is found in a two-thousand-year-old legend which depicts the angels in heaven bursting into joyous song when the Israelites crossed the Red Sea successfully. "The Holy

One rebuked the angels: 'My children, the Egyptians, are drowning and you dare sing!' "

Are Jews Forbidden to Drink Hard Liquor?

THE Jewish attitude towards drinking is a key to the whole broad concept of how best to cope with problems of vice, temptation and sin. Prohibitionists try to solve these problems by removing the instruments of vice. Without alcohol, they maintain, there will be no alcoholics. Judaism considers this approach both superficial and ineffective. Our tradition would urge that we look, not at the sin, but at the sinner.

Drunkenness is regarded as an offense against man and God, not because of its own inherent ugliness, but because it is a symptom of a serious character defect—the lack of self-control. A person who has developed the art of self-restraint in other aspects of his life will practice moderation in eating and drinking as well.

Thus, drinking liquor is not forbidden—but drunkenness is sharply condemned. Students of Jewish family life have frequently observed that intoxicating drinks can be found in nearly every Jewish home, but drunkenness is nevertheless a rarity.

Actually, a moderate indulgence in wine or other spirits is quite in keeping with the Jewish tradition. The Bible speaks of a little wine "rejoicing the heart." Every joyous event—birth, marriage, Bar Mitzvah and numerous holy days—include wine as part of the celebration. The ancient rabbis deprecated austerity as unhealthy for the soul. "Be not righteous overmuch,' the Bible wisely suggests.

Apparently this tolerant judgment was sustained by centuries of experience. The incidence of acute alcoholism among Jews is far below the average of the general community, is in fact an almost unheard-of disease. And more significantly, several of the by-products of drunkenness, crimes of violence, destitution and broken homes, are also far rarer in Jewish life.

Our tradition shares the view of the modern psychiatrist that a happy, well-adjusted human being will not seek in liquor the satisfactions he can find in more creative and worthwhile goals.

Do Jews Believe in 'Luck'?

MANY of the ancient rabbis felt that "luck" often plays an important role in shaping our lives. The phrase *mazol tov*, "congratulations," reflects this thought. *Mazol tov*—the traditional greeting at weddings, circumcisions, anniversaries and all occasions of family festivity, means literally "lucky star." Thus, in the greeting is a wish that the event being celebrated take place "under a lucky star."

During the early days of Jewish history, there seems to have been an accepted belief that human destiny was in some way linked to the motion of the stars. The prophet Jeremiah was among the first to condemn this notion as pagan, and centuries later Moses Maimonides renewed the attack on astrology. But long after the origin of the phrase was lost, *mazol tov* continued to mean, "May your life be crowned with good fortune."

Yet, Judaism is not a fatalistic religion. The Jews rejected the belief, popular among the ancient Greeks and followers of certain Oriental faiths, that man has no control over his own destiny. The ancient rabbis maintained: "Everything is foreseen, yet freedom of choice is given."

The age-old dilemma of reconciling God's all-knowing

nature with man's responsibility for his own acts is not easy to resolve. One of the rabbis suggested that the *first* ethical decision in any situation lies in our hands. From then on, "one good deed leads to another, one evil deed to a second." Thus, for good or for evil, the original choice is ours.

What Is the Jewish Attitude Towards Censorship?

THERE is no word for censorship in classical Hebrew and little precedent for the practice in ancient Jewish traditions.

In medieval times, however, the atmosphere of censorship which permeated the western world did not leave Judaism untouched. Some religious leaders denounced the reading of books which "raised doubts" in the minds of the faithful. A few overzealous rabbis forbade their followers to study the liberal writings of Moses Maimonides. In the seventeenth century, the philosophers Baruch Spinoza and Uriel da Costa, both religious radicals, suffered the blows of intolerance from their own religious brethren.

But in more recent times we have returned to the Jewish tradition that censorship of any kind is not a constructive force in character development. Sound moral character, we feel, does not grow out of avoiding those ideas and concepts with which we do not agree, but rather out of learning to choose from the open market place of human thought those concepts which are creative and worthwhile.

There is, understandably, a kind of censorship which educators exercise in the choice of lesson materials. But this is based on selection rather than suppression. Maimonides, for example, remarked that teaching philosophy to the immature was like feeding steak to an infant. Nothing is wrong with either the food or the child; there is just no point in offering him something which he cannot digest. Even during the darkest days of suppression, when Rabbi Solomon ben Adret (1305 A.D.) issued a ban against Greek science and philosophy, the prohibition applied only to those Jews who had not yet reached their twenty-fifth birthday.

How Does Judaism Regard Psychiatry?

THERE is a Jewish prayer for a friend or relative who is ill which reads: "May God so endow the attending physician with insight and skill that our friend be soon fully restored to health . . ." The "insight and skill" of the doctor is as much a gift of God as any other aptitude possessed by man.

Judaism is sympathetic towards any science which promotes health and well-being. Psychiatry has proved itself a valuable segment of such science, and Judaism does not reject it. We do not, of course, regard psychiatry as infallible, for it is, with all its insights, a human science. But its objectives—the development of happier, fuller, maturer human beings—are unquestionably in consonance with the spirit of Judaism.

Modern dynamic psychology has given new tools to the physician in his battle against one of mankind's greatest scourges: the diseases of the mind. Above all, it has given us an understanding of man's inner conflicts which has helped erase the prejudice and shame attached to mental illness. The science of psychiatry has imbued modern man with sensitivity and compassion that replace long centuries of superstition, ignorance and fear. We cannot consider such a contribution in conflict with religious teaching.

The late Rabbi Joshua Loth Liebman was an outstanding exponent of the view that Judaism and psychiatry are ideal partners. In his introduction to *Psychiatry and Religion*, Dr. Liebman listed four goals in the "attainment of a new maturity by the men and women of our age." A mature human being, he explained, accepts life as full of tension; he is not tormented by childish guilt feelings but avoids adult sin; he can give up immediate pleasures for long-range values; and, finally, he is reconciled to the fact that he cannot accomplish everything in life.

These and many other objectives of modern psychiatry are clearly echoed in the early teachings of Judaism. The rabbis in the academies of Babylonia and Jabneh had never heard of conditioned reflexes, complexes or neuroses. But they gave the people of the second, third and fourth centuries profound psychological insights nonetheless. The ancient academicians understood fully the concept of maturity. Commenting on the repetitious verse in Exodus: "And the child grew up . . . And Moses grew up . . ." a rabbi explained: "The first referred to Moses' physical growth—the second to his mental growth." The men of the *Talmud* obviously knew that in healthy growth psychological development kept pace with the development of the body.

To those whom today's psychologists would call "compulsive," Rabbi Tarphon recommended cryptically, "Thine is not the duty to finish the task—but neither art thou free to desist from it."

"Be not righteous overmuch" and "Be not evil in thine own esteem" are other examples of sound psychological advice offered by the ancient rabbis. Judaism set its standards high—but not utterly out of reach—and thus tended to avoid morbid guilt feelings. "For there liveth no man that sinneth not," the Bible said, and though saintliness was extolled in our tradition, it was not demanded of the average human being.

The ancient rabbis also realized that we are not always the best judges of ourselves. "If one man call thee a donkey, heed it not—if two men call thee, get thee a saddle!"

What Is the Jewish Attitude Toward Suicide?

THROUGHOUT the Jewish tradition runs the belief that life is only lent to us. Rabbi Hananiah, a great Jewish martyr who was burned at the stake during the Roman persecution, is said to have refused to remove the wet cloth placed in his mouth by his tormentors, although to do so would have hastened his death and ended his horrible agony. To his pleading disciples he explained, "My life is not my own to give or to take. It is His, alone."

Legal euthanasia—or mercy killing at the request of someone incurably ill and in pain—is also against our tradition. For in this case, another person is being used as an instrument of suicide.

Like most other religions, Judaism deals harshly with the proven suicide. A Jew who takes his own life is buried without honor or eulogy and is mourned without the traditional ceremonials.

However, we are urged not to come to rash conclusions

when we are faced with apparent self-destruction. The Hebrew phrase for "suicide" suggests that only a person who has temporarily lost his reason would succumb to such an impulse. In line with the talmudic dictum, "Give every man the benefit of the doubt," Jewish tradition provides that no person may be deemed a suicide unless there is overwhelming evidence that it was the deliberate act of a man or woman of sound mind. If there is a shadow of doubt, we must assume that the act was accidental, or at least beyond the control of the victim.

Why Do Jews Concern Themselves with the Rights of Other Minority Groups?

JEWS have often been the victims of tyranny and oppression. Their familiarity with cruel and arbitrary rulers dates back to the days of the Pharaohs. It is a primary tenet of Judaism to fight against the mistreatment of any human being, whatever his race, religion or ancestry may be.

Some people who have been unjustly treated are embittered by their experience and hit back by lashing out against others, weaker than themselves, whenever they have the chance. The Jewish people, on the other hand, have reacted to their own suffering with a deep sensitivity to the pain of others.

Sympathy for the misfortunes of their fellow human beings has become a part of the Jewish way of life. Kindness to strangers is a constant theme in the Old Testament, with the frequent admonition to "remember you were strangers in the land of Egypt."

The ancient prophets of Israel, twenty-six hundred years ago, were among the first to preach love of strangers. It was Amos who cautioned the people of Israel against the universal temptation to feel superior to other peoples. " 'Are you not as the Ethiopians unto me?' said the Lord."

Through the years, history has added self-interest to moral convictions. For Jews know that tyranny is infectious—that as long as one minority group can be made the scapegoat for other people's social and economic ills, no group is safe. The *Talmud* tells the story of three men in a boat. One began to drill a hole under his seat. When his companions pleaded with him to stop, he asked: "What are you worrying about? I'm only drilling under *my* seat." And the moral drawn by the ancient rabbis has been repeated many, many times over: "We're *all* in the same boat."

Are American Jews Returning to Religion?

A "RETURN TO RELIGION" may take several forms. For greater clarity, the question might therefore be divided into three separate parts:

Is there an increased trend toward traditionalism—toward the Orthodox *forms* of the ancestral faith?

Is there a marked increase in synagogue participation or affiliation?

Is there a movement toward greater spiritual emphasis—a heightened idealism and a rejection of materialism?

The answer to the first part of the question is not easy. Reform Judaism reports that many of the rituals and ceremonies of Orthodoxy have found their way to Reform congregations. Recent studies by Professors Marshall Sklare, Sidney Goldstein and Theodore Lenn verify this trend toward traditionalism. There has been a decline in such observances as dietary laws and strict Sabbath practices. But many more American Jews are lighting Sabbath and Hanukkah candles (a marked increase in the latter); they celebrate the Passover *Seder*; provide their children with some form of religious instruction; maintain ties with Israel, than a decade ago. The number of children receiving intensive Jewish education and participating in religiously-oriented camp experience has increased dramatically.

The answer to the second question is also not too readily available, especially since Orthodox bodies will not release any statistical information. There is no doubt that synagogue affiliation reached an all-time high during the post-World War II years. Many new congregations were established, especially in Long Island, New York, the north shore of Chicago, and the suburbs of Los Angeles. Established congregations experienced a remarkable growth and hundreds of millions of dollars were spent on new synagogue buildings. The national religious bodies expanded rapidly. The three major seminaries, whose individual annual budgets in the early 1950's were little more than a million dollars each, reached ten million dollars in the 1970's.

Unfortunately, statistics in this field are not detailed. We have no way of judging which of the three groups has had the fastest growth. In addition, synagogue statistics are naturally based on affiliation—on belonging rather than believing. Some Jewish community studies suggest that approximately 55 per cent of American Jews regard themselves as Conservative, 25 per cent as Reform and 15 per cent as Orthodox. The most remarkable gains in recent years seem to be among the more traditional congregations.

One authority estimates that approximately forty per cent of the Jewish population—a smaller percentage than Roman Catholics; higher than Protestants—belong to congregations. This figure, however, does not include many who have no formal synagogue affiliation but attend some religious functions, send their children to Sunday School and use synagogue facilities for weddings and funerals.

Is there a return to the faith of our fathers in a personal sense, in terms of individual commitment, belief in God, acceptance of the Moral Law, and attachment to the Jewish way of life? Here we venture into the realm of pure conjecture. Few studies have been made, and, quite possibily, none can be made with any degree of validity. For my part, I would hazard the belief that more Jews are searching for identity than ever before. The wanton murder of six million Jews in a single decade has aroused among those who survived a natural impulse to close ranks spiritually, and to search for meaning in historic faith. The restlessness of our atomic age, too, has prompted some Jews to seek strength in their religious roots.

❦ [III] ❧

MARRIAGE AND THE FAMILY

As together you now drink from this cup,
So may you, under God's guidance,
In perfect union and devotion to each other,
Draw contentment, comfort and felicity
From the cup of life;
Thereby may you find life's joys doubly gladdening,
Its bitterness sweetened,
And all things hallowed
By true companionship and love.

THE MARRIAGE RITUAL

Marriage and the Family

Most of our attitudes towards life are born in the family circle. In spite of the intrusions upon the attention of the child, by his playmates, the school, the radio, movies and television —even the religious school—it is the home which provides most of his basic values and ideals. The auxiliary influences modify, but they rarely determine the essential standards which the child acquires in the living room, dining room and kitchen of his home.

The Jewish home is not unique in its emphasis on family integrity. The French home, we know, is the heart of the nation. The Norwegians, the Dutch, the Italians, all pride themselves in their love of family. Every religious, national and cultural tradition has made the family the cornerstone of its existence.

But Judaism, as we shall see, has created scores of family rites and ceremonies that have linked *religious* loyalties to love of home and has strengthened both the home and the religion in the process.

Judaism measures the dignity of man in relation to his family circle: respect and consideration for parents and grandparents; mutual regard in the husband-wife relationship; recognition of the rights of the child. The Jewish home is not lacking in authority, but it is far from authoritarian. Each member of the family has an important—an indispensable role. Together they carry on the continuity of their family and their religion.

Probably the most characteristic feature of the Jewish home is its emphasis on the *unity* of family experience—the *togetherness* of family life. The *Talmud* suggests that parents are to share joys and sorrows alike with their children. If a neighbor's family was bereaved, they were to be visited by parents *with* their children. At weddings and other joyous events, children traditionally accompanied their elders. Children learned the facts of life and death naturally and directly—and the family remained intact.

Today, modern Jewish families, along with many of their non-Jewish neighbors, have streamlined some of the traditional family customs. But most of them retain the high standards and the important group values which will always be worth preserving.

Is It True That in Judaism the Home Is More Important Than the Synagogue?

YES, definitely. If all Jewish houses of worship were to close, Jewish religious life would continue intact, because the center of Jewish religious life is the home.

Rabbi Elijah of Vilna, probably the most outstanding Jewish scholar of the eighteenth century, advised his sons to recite their daily prayers at home rather than in the synagogue. The synagogue, he felt, offered numerous distractions when there were no scheduled Sabbath or Holy Day services. But in his own home the worshiper could achieve true communion with God.

Jews regard their home as a religious sanctuary. The family is the fountainhead of Jewish worship, and our religious ritual is as much a matter for the home as it is for the synagogue. The mother, lighting the Sabbath candles on Friday evenings; the father, blessing his children at the Sabbath table; the dozens of happy, meaningful rituals that surround the observance of every Jewish holiday; the scroll proclaiming love of God (*mezuzah*) on the doorpost—these are an integral part of the total Jewish ritual and ceremony. Our religion is essentially a family religion and many of our deepest religious ties are also familial. A Jewish G.I. on active duty is more likely to observe Passover, because of its intimate home associations, than the more sacred Day of Atonement.

Mishpachah, the Hebrew word for family, refers not only to parents and children, but to a social unit which includes aunts, uncles and even the remotest of cousins. Such intimacy has its obvious disadvantages. Privacy in the sense of intimacies unshared by *mishpachah* is not easy to achieve. But these family ties have made juvenile delinquency somewhat of a rarity among Jews.

The Catholic weekly, *America*, glowingly observes that "the disproportionately small number of Jewish children requiring public care is a tribute to the good state of Jewish family life." The Jesuit magazine considered "family solidarity" as one of the four outstanding characteristics of American Jews (the other three: temperance, industry and zeal for education).

This "family solidarity" has been a major factor in the survival of Judaism through the trials and tribulations of the centuries. The Jewish home has always provided a kind of portable religion that could be readily sustained as long as the family existed.

Are There Special Ceremonies Involved in the Engagement?

TRADITIONALLY, an elaborate, centuries-old ritual solemnized the Jewish betrothal. Formal documents, called *tenaim,* recorded the engagement and only a divorce could terminate the agreement. Today, of course, there is less formality and rigidity to Jewish betrothal ceremonies, but they are generally marked with festivity by Jews everywhere.

Among the Jews of India, a marriage entails three distinct rituals: espousal, betrothal, and marriage. The first takes place immediately after parental agreement. Five female friends of the bride march to her home carrying a plateful of sugar which they drop into the mouths of the girl and her mother, chanting "In the name of the Lord."

The engagement ceremony of the Indian Jew is celebrated with much pageantry: The groom rides to the bride's home on a gaily bedecked horse; and in an involved ring ceremony he announces three times to his prospective bride: "Behold thou are betrothed unto me with this ring according to the law of Moses and Israel." The bride's father then presents his future son-in-law with a ring, and a sweet repast follows.

Jewish custom suggests that engagements be neither too long nor short. Maimonides, a twelfth-century forerunner of today's medical marriage counsellor, cautioned that a protracted engagement is not wholesome, especially if the young couple has reached physical maturity. But he also warned against too brief an engagement which, he pointed out, is frequently a prelude to an impulsive marriage.

The current popularity of double-ring rites has some interesting antecedents. In medieval Germany and other countries, only the groom wore an engagement ring; among Turkish and Greek Jews, it was only the girl. The custom of resplendent rings adorning both the young man and his fiancee appears to have originated in jewelry-loving Italy.

Is There Any Special Meaning to the Various Symbols Used in a Jewish Wedding?

MANY of the customs connected with the marriage ceremony are largely a matter of local practice rather than of Jewish law. In each country where Jews have settled they have adopted, in addition to their required religious rites, some of the non-religious customs of their non-Jewish neighbors. Processionals, attendants and order of procession are matters of custom rather than law.

There are, however, certain traditional rites and symbols connected with most Jewish weddings. These include the canopy (*chupah*) under which the marriage vows are taken; the cup of wine from which bride and groom both sip at the beginning and end of the ceremony; the simple, unadorned wedding band; and the religious marriage document, called a *Kethubah*. In most Jewish ceremonies there is also a ritual shat-

tering of the wine glass after the bride and groom have tasted
the wine together, though the modern Reform ritual has eliminated this, along with the canopy, the marriage document and
the second cup of wine.

Each of these traditional symbols is endowed with a variety
of meanings. The canopy lends an atmosphere of royalty to the
occasion—for the bride and groom are considered king and
queen on their wedding day. It is also a symbol of the privacy
to which the newly-wed couple is entitled. In the traditional
ceremony, the bride and groom are permitted to leave the
wedding guests for a few moments of unchaperoned privacy—
a welcome breather for the two who are so overwhelmed by
scores of relatives and friends.

The ring—which need not be made of gold—is a symbol of
perfection and eternity, the circle without beginning or end.
The emphasis on simplicity in the ring is typical of the Jewish
tradition of equality. For an unadorned ring minimizes the difference between a poor and a wealthy bridal pair. The giving
of a ring without stones is, however, a matter of custom, not of
law.

The sharing of a single cup of wine by the bride and groom
is a reminder of their common destiny, for henceforth their
lives will be inseparable. Originally, the first cup, at the open-
ing of the marriage rites, represented the betrothal or engagement, and the second the actual marriage. Today we frequently refer to the first as the cup of joy, which is even more
joyous because it is shared. The second is the cup of sacrifice.
The burdens which fall upon man and wife are lightened when
two deeply devoted people bear equal measure.

The breaking of the glass climaxes the traditional service and
is interpreted in many ways. Some consider it a vestige of
primitive magic. Among many ancient tribes, a loud noise was

used on joyous occasions to frighten away evil spirits jealous of human happiness. But Jewish tradition maintains that the broken glass is a reminder of the destruction of the temple, a symbol of the sorrows of Israel. The bridal couple, in the midst of their personal happiness, are reminded of the sorrows of life and sobered by the thought of their responsibilities.

Judaism insists that marriage is not just a private matter, but one in which the entire community has a stake. In old European Jewish communities, for example, every wedding was more than a family affair. If a bride was too poor to afford a trousseau, a collection was made on the eve of the Sabbath and the girl was outfitted. No wedding invitations were sent out, because the entire community considered it a religious obligation to attend, bless the couple and comment on the radiant beauty of the bride.

Tradition has it that a solemn obligation rests upon every wedding guest to tell the groom he has chosen the loveliest of brides. The ancient rabbis were a little disturbed about this practice. If, even by the wildest stretch of imagination, the description did not fit the bride, wouldn't the guest be violating the Commandment against bearing false witness? But the wise rabbis found their answer: *every* bride is beautiful on her wedding day. And in her bridegroom's eyes, she is without peer.

Does the Jewish Religion Allow Birth Control or Abortion?

THE Jewish religion has traditionally been opposed to birth control or abortion when practiced for purely selfish reasons. A home without children, Jews believe, is a home without blessing. Man's highest fulfillment is in his children and his family life. According to Jewish law, every man and wife have a solemn obligation to bring at least two children into the world.

However, Judaism has always sanctioned birth control under certain conditions—such as where pregnancy represents a health hazard to the mother or child, or when previous children have been born defective. Modern Judaism has extended this concept to include extreme poverty, inadequate living conditions and threats to the welfare of existing children in the family. The Central Conference of American Rabbis (Reform) goes so far as to declare that birth control is a necessity under certain family conditions. "We urge the recommendation of the members of intelligent birth regulation." (Adopted in 1930.) Most Reform and some Conservative rabbis subscribe to the program of planned parenthood.

A closely related issue is that of therapeutic abortion, prescribed by a physician to save the life or health of a pregnant woman. In Jewish law such an action is considered entirely justified. The life of the mother, Jews believe, is more important than that of the child not yet born, both to her husband and to any other children she may have.

The most important consideration in both questions is: what is best for the entire family? The sanctity of marriage is not in reproduction. It is in the bond that exists between husband, wife and the children they want and love.

Do Jews Value a Boy Child More Than a Girl?

MODERN Jews, like modern parents of every faith, place equal value on all their children, whether boys or girls. But in ancient days, the Jews, like all patriarchal societies, considered the birth of a son a greater blessing than that of a daughter.

Sons were a great economic asset to the family for they helped with the fields and with all the manual labor and they remained an integral part of the family after they grew up. They could be depended upon to take over the father's responsibilities and to provide for their parents in their old age. From an Orthodox ritual viewpoint, it is the son, not the daughter, who recites the Kaddish after a parent's death.

Daughters, on the other hand, were somewhat of a liability. They had to be guarded and protected; and when they were grown they married and became a part of their husband's family, taking with them the dowry their parents had to provide.

In Eastern Europe the responsibilities of the parents often did not stop when their daughters were married. If circumstances permitted, they often supported their sons-in-law as well for several years while the young men continued their studies—a kind of son-in-law Bill of Rights under which promising young scholars could marry and enjoy a subsistence allowance while learning.

There was also among our ancestors the feeling sometimes echoed by feminists today that men lived a far less circumscribed life than their sisters. In the old Orthodox ritual a man recited a special blessing each morning thanking God that he had not been made a woman, while a woman prayed: "Thank God that He fashioned me according to His will."

Who Names the Baby in Jewish Families?

THIS is another question wrapped up in custom and superstition, rather than in religious law. Theoretically, the name of the baby is the father's decision. If there is a choice between the name of the father's father and that of the mother's father, the paternal grandfather usually has preference. However, in some countries it is the mother's prerogative to name the first-born.

In America and many European countries, children are frequently given both a Hebrew name after a relative, and one common to the land of their birth. However, there is no basis for this in Jewish law. Boy babies are named on the eighth day, at the time of circumcision. If circumcision is postponed, the naming of the baby is also delayed. A common superstition, years ago, was to put off naming the child as long as possible, especially when the infant was frail, since it was believed that a death summons could not be delivered without a name.

Among the Ashkenazic Jews a baby girl is named on the first Sabbath, when the mother is well enough to attend a synagogue. In Rome, the infant herself is brought before the altar of the synagogue to be blessed by the rabbi. Among Orthodox and Conservative Jews in the United States, a baby girl is named by the father in the synagogue on the Sabbath following the birth.

The blessing pronounced over the head of the new-born Jewish child is three-fold: May he grow in vigor of mind and body for *Torah*, to be an intelligent and informed human being; for *chupah*, to reach the marriage canopy; and for a *life of good deeds*.

Do Jews Always Name a Child After a Deceased Relative?

THE custom of naming a child after a relative who has died exists only among the Ashkenazic Jews of Eastern and Central Europe. Among the Sephardic or Mediterranean Jews, children are quite often named after living grandparents.

In Jewish tradition, the name given to a child always has some meaning. To call a boy Abraham is to associate it with the kindliness of the patriarch Abraham. A girl is called Ruth in the hope that she will live up to the loyalty and devotion of the biblical Ruth. Parents do not name a child after a ne'er-do-well relative, because they do not want to associate the youngster with the kinsman's blemishes. For the same reason, a child is not named after a brother or sister who died in childhood or early youth.

In ancient times it was customary to give children names entirely unrelated to those of relatives, living *or* dead. Jacob, for example, did not name any of his children or grandchildren Abraham or Isaac. Perhaps it was then felt that naming a child after an ancestor would mean that the older person might be forgotten as people began to associate the name with the young child.

The custom of not using the name of a living relative dates back to a superstition of the Middle Ages. It was thought that the angel of death, appearing with a summons, might serve it on the child instead of on the older relative and so bring about premature death.

Even though the rabbis recognized this fear as based on superstition, they made no attempt to discourage the custom, since it had some practical value. When two members of the family bear the same name it can lead to confusion. There were many reasons, though, to encourage memorializing the name of an honored grandparent, uncle or aunt, whose qualities the parents would like to see reborn in their child.

Do Jews Believe in Strict Parental Discipline?

APPARENTLY the problem of how best to bring up children is both ageless and universal. The literature of antiquity is full of references to parent-child relationships.

Patience and an understanding of the mind of the child was the keynote of most talmudic advice to parents. "Don't become impatient with your child because he wants so much— and hardly notices how many sacrifices you are making for him," wrote Bahya ibn Pakuda in the eleventh century.

The most important factor in child rearing, it was stressed, was the general home atmosphere. Rabbi Nachman of Bratzlav, one of the great Hasidic teachers, warned that a home in which parents quarrel will not produce good children. In the long run, he declared, "We have the kind of children we deserve."

The Bible counsels, "Spare the rod and spoil the child." But the rabbis of the *Talmud* did not interpret this injunction too seriously: "A father should not permit a spirit of fear to prevail in his home," taught Rabbi Hisda. And other rabbis added: "If you must strike a child, do it with the string of a shoe."

Of course there are occasions in normal family life, the rabbis recognized, when it is necessary to discipline the child. But Jewish tradition stressed that the child must never be made to feel that he is unloved. The way must be left open for reconciliation and understanding. "Reprove the child with your left hand, and draw him closer with your right," declares the *Talmud*. "Children are the gift of God," our tradition maintains, and parents are only His trustees.

A contemporary rabbi, Isidore Epstein, carries out this thought in his book, *The Jewish Way of Life*. "Parents do not derive their authority because they are stronger, or older or possessors of material goods. Nor do they deserve particular reverence because they happen to be the originators of their children's life," he declares. The only authority they possess, Rabbi Epstein explains, grows out of their responsibilities to their children and to God.

The stereotype of the stern and austere parent of ancient Judaism is far from accurate. The *Talmud* tells the story of a man whose will contained the extraordinary provision that his son was to inherit the estate when "he became a fool." The son sought the advice of two scholars who took him to the home of the learned Rabbi Joshua. When the three men arrived at the rabbi's house, they saw him crawling around on his hands and knees with a stick in his mouth, capering with his young son. When asked about the will, the wise rabbi answered, "You already have the explanation." The father wanted his son to inherit the estate when he, himself, became a father and enjoyed silly games with his children.

The key to character training lies beyond the narrow road of discipline. Judaism would agree with Aristotle that sound moral training consists in developing healthy habits of thought and action. But these habits grow out of parental example rather than parental moralizing. A disciple of another great Hasidic rabbi tried to impress his teacher with the announcement that he prayed daily that his sons would study *Torah* faithfully. The rabbi pointedly remarked that if the man prayed without engaging in study himself, his children would imitate him: they, too, would pray that their children be learned, without any learning on their part. "The teaching is not what counts," says the *Talmud*. "It is the doing that is important." And an eighteenth-century rabbi summed up this thought with the moving advice: "Every Jew should so conduct himself that his son will proudly say: 'The God of my father.'"

Does Jewish Religious Law Permit the Marriage of Relatives?

THE Book of Leviticus contains a series of restrictions against the marriage of blood relatives, as well as of certain relatives by marriage. For example, a man may not marry his aunt, or the widow of his son. But if the law of the state permits, Jewish law raises no objection to a marriage of first cousins, or of uncle and niece. In fact, in the nineteenth century in Europe, such family alliances were twice as prevalent among Jews as among non-Jews. This was largely because in small Jewish communities the choice of a mate was naturally limited, and the tendency was for relatives to marry each other rather than to marry outside their faith.

According to the *Talmud*, "the law of the land is Jewish law." It is a religious obligation to adhere to state laws, even if they conflict with accepted Jewish tradition. This principle does not apply when it involves a violation of the Mosaic law, or the moral code. But in such matters as marriage, Jews are under *religious* obligation to observe "the law of the land."

In Biblical times, a childless widow was required to marry her husband's brother, in order to preserve intact the family property. This was known as "levirate marriage." Release from this obligation entailed a special ceremony akin to divorce. The law was gradually modified, and finally, several centuries ago, the rabbis issued a ban against this type of marriage. The Orthodox group has preserved a vestige of the old law by continuing to require the ceremony of release.

What Is the Jewish Attitude Toward Divorce?

DIVORCE has always been rare in the Jewish community. It is still well below the national average in the United States. Nevertheless, when differences between husband and wife make living together intolerable, Judaism not only permits divorce—it encourages it. A love-filled home, our teachers tell us, is a sanctuary; a loveless home is a sacrilege.

In the strict letter of Jewish law, divorce is easy to obtain (though this has no bearing on the civil divorce requirements of most countries). The *Talmud* says you can divorce your wife if she burns your supper. As one of the rabbis explains, if burned roast takes on such great importance, there must be a basic incompatibility that might best be dealt with directly.

The emphasis always is on reconciliation and a better understanding between husband and wife. And Jewish couples seldom consider divorce hastily or capriciously—particularly when there are children. For it is the children who must then pay most heavily for their parents' mistake. "The parents eat sour grapes and the teeth of the children are set on edge," declared Ezekiel.

But in the Jewish tradition it is considered a greater evil for youngsters to be reared in a home without peace and mutual respect than to have to face their parents' divorce. When two people can find no common basis to continue their marriage despite repeated and genuine efforts, Judaism both sanctions and approves their divorce.

A divorced person is encouraged to remarry. Jewish tradition frowns on the unmarried state, for those without mates "may come to sin or the thought of sin."

What Is the Role of the Wife and Mother in the Jewish Family? In Religious Life?

EVERY Sabbath eve, the observant Jewish family recites the last chapter of Proverbs—a tribute to the ideal wife and mother.

The virtues extolled in these twenty-two verses spell out the qualities of a perfect wife. She is a reverent human being, efficient, understanding, buoyantly optimistic, openhearted in helping the needy who knock at her gate and, above all, the kind of person upon whom the entire family can lean.

From the biblical Book of Proverbs to the modern Jewish folk ballad, the wife and mother has been depicted as the epitome of tender devotion, selflessness and loyalty to her faith. The mother sets the spiritual tone in family life; she is most responsible for the character development of her children; and she holds the family together in the face of adversity.

Jewish tradition makes few formal ritual demands on the woman in synagogue life. But she assumes full responsibility for the atmosphere of piety and reverence in the home and for the inculcation of Jewish ideals. She gathers her children around her on the eve of the Sabbath to hear her pronounce the blessing over the lights. She prepares the home for each festival and creates a mood of joyous expectancy in the household.

In the old Jewish communities, the training of the children up to the age of six was vested in the mother's hands, so that in these impressionable years she could teach her youngsters lasting values. But more important was her traditional role of counselor to the entire family. The *Talmud* says: "No matter how short your wife is, lean down and take her advice."

In the year 1620, a Jewish philosopher named Isaac of Posen wrote a little book for his daughter that was a best seller among Jewish women of the seventeenth century. The book, which went through nineteen editions before the turn of the century, was called *The Good Heart*, and included among its chapters ten commandments on how to be a good wife:

1. Be careful when your husband is angry—be neither gay nor cross—just smile and speak softly.
2. Don't keep him waiting for his meals. Hunger is the father of anger.
3. Don't wake him when he's sleeping.
4. Be careful of his money; don't keep any money matters from him.
5. Keep his secrets secret. If he boasts, keep that secret too.
6. Don't like his enemies or hate his friends.
7. Don't disagree with him or suggest that your advice is better than his.
8. Don't expect the impossible from him.
9. If you heed his requests, he will turn out to be your slave.
10. Don't say anything that will hurt him. If you treat him like a king, he will treat you like a queen.

The sages of Judaism also had advice for husbands as well. "How can a man be assured of having a blessed home? By respecting his wife."

✵ [IV] ✵

RELIGIOUS LAW
AND RITUAL

*It matters not whether
you do much or little
so long as your heart
is directed toward
Heaven.*

TALMUD

Religious Law and Ritual

ONE of the most distinctive features of Judaism is its great variety of rites and ceremonies—rituals that cover every aspect of life from the cradle to the grave. The Jewish religion is replete with symbols of all kinds. And while a few are the accumulation of recent centuries, most of them have very ancient origins.

At first glance, these symbols suggest some inconsistency in Judaism. On the one hand this religion divests the idea of God of any physical form, and rejects all imagery. The use of statues or pictures in worship is forbidden. There is a ban on perpetuating the physical memories of the patriarchs, prophets and rabbis. But on the other hand, tradition has multiplied symbol upon symbol to represent the ideals of Judaism.

The paradox resolves itself quite readily. Jews are forbidden to think of God in any physical image, for God is pure Spirit. But the leaders and architects of the Jewish faith realized that symbols enrich not only our enjoyment of life, but our understanding of it as well.

Every human relation, every human aspiration, every great emotion, means more to us if it is clothed in some symbolic act. The awe and the mystery surrounding birth, maturity and, finally, death evoke feelings that are almost inexpressible. They represent a complex of experience encompassing all the beauty, the goodness, the worthwhileness of life. Judaism uses a single word, *holiness*, to express this symphony of emotions.

At every juncture in our lives touched by holiness, a symbol or rite helps to give some concrete expression. This is true not only in religious matters: the engagement ring marks the love of two young people; the flag represents all the love and devotion of a man for his country.

Religious symbols and rituals serve a similar purpose. We sanctify life, according to Jewish tradition, when we pause in the midst of our experiences to relate it to the Source of our Being.

When parents bring their child to the synagogue for Bar Mitzvah or Confirmation, emotions run deep. There is joy in the contemplation of a youngster growing into manhood or womanhood; and there is parental pride as they see their boy or girl assume a role in the life of the synagogue. The young man or woman also feels a sense of reverence at taking on the first responsibilities of adulthood. In the ceremonial of Bar Mitzvah and Confirmation there is an outlet for all these emotions.

To say such ceremonies are superfluous is to say that words can get along without music. They can, of course. But music often adds a quality which marks the difference between the casual and the significant, the humdrum and the exalted. So rites and symbols frequently lend poetry to life and make it more worth living.

The Hebrew word for holy is *kodosh*, and it is found in various forms throughout the Jewish ritual.

On Sabbath and festivals the Jew recites the Kiddush, the Sanctification over wine. The words and the blessing are not as meaningful as the ceremony itself. The father holds the silver cup in hand and chants the words aloud; the mother and children listen attentively and respond with a closing "Amen." It is a simple act—yet it mirrors all of the beauty and serenity which the Sabbath represents.

The ritual of Silent Devotion, recited three times daily, contains a prayer called the Kedushah, in which the worshiper repeats the words of the prophet, "Holy, holy, holy, is the Lord of hosts, the whole world is filled with His glory."

And, at the end of life, there is another form of sanctification, the Kaddish (see p. 96)—the mourner's affirmation that despite his affliction, life is sacred and worthwhile.

The late Rabbi Milton Steinberg often spoke of the consolation which the Kaddish prayer afforded him. Life had meaning for him, he told his congregation, because it had a holy spirit in it. That is why, despite its wonderful treasures, *"It is easier for me to let go. For these things are not and never have been mine. They belong to the Universe and the God who stands behind it. True, I have been privileged to enjoy them for an hour but they were always a loan to be recalled.*

"And I let go of them the more easily because I know that as parts of the divine economy they will not be lost. The sunset, the bird's song, the baby's smile, the thunder of music, the surge of great poetry, the dreams of the heart, and my own being, dear to me as every man's is to him, all these I can well trust to Him who made them. There is poignancy and regret about giving them up, but no anxiety. When they slip from my hands they will pass to hands better, stronger and wiser than mine. . . .

"Life is dear, let us then hold it tight while yet we may; but we must hold it loosely also! . . . For only when He is given, can we hold life at once infinitely precious and yet a thing lightly to be surrendered. Only because of Him is it made possible for us to clasp the world, but with relaxed hands; to embrace it, but with open arms."

Is There One Book of Jewish Law?

No SINGLE book embodies all the religious laws binding upon Jews.

The closest anyone has come to compiling a single legal code, is the *Shulchan Aruch*, a sixteenth-century work by Joseph Caro. This book contains the basic law which today guides most Orthodox Jews in the western world. But though Orthodox Jews accept most of the *Shulchan Aruch*, they still do not consider it the full body of Jewish law—which consists of 'all the accepted codes, commentaries, amendments, responsa (rabbinic answers to problems arising from actual experience) that are to be found in the entire library of Jewish learning.

Reform Jews, however, do not accept the *Shulchan Aruch* as binding, and Conservative Jews also no longer abide by a number of its regulations.

Another standard legal work is the Code of Maimonides, which sets down, systematically and logically, the conflicting opinions of the *Talmud*.

In recent years, some Reform Jews have expressed the need for a standard code of Reform practice. But there are many who fear that any form of standardization would defeat the very liberation which Reform Judaism stands for.

For the same reason, Conservative Judaism has also not created a single book of law, which many Conservative Jews believe would stunt the natural growth and evolution in Judaism.

Even the Bible cannot be considered the unchanging standard for religious practice. The biblical laws concerning polygamy, interest, tithing, slavery and a score of other subjects have been reinterpreted out of existence. In this sense, rabbinical law and the Bible are not identical. A Jew who followed the biblical command of Levirate marriage (see p. 65) would be violating the rabbinical law which forbids that practice.

Is There a Priesthood in Judaism?

THERE is no priesthood in Judaism that parallels the Roman or Greek institution in Christianity. However, Orthodox and Conservative Jews still regard the descendants of Aaron, brother of Moses and first High Priest of the Temple after the Exodus, as priests, Cohanim, with limited functions in religious life.

A Jew bearing the name of Cohen, Kohn, Katz, Kahn or Kaplan is probably a descendant of Aaron, though this is not always true, because some people have adopted these names to streamline more complicated surnames.

A Cohen (one of the Cohanim) is in no sense a clergyman. But by virtue of his illustrious heredity, he enjoys certain religious privileges and has several specific ritual tasks. During the reading of the *Torah* on the Sabbath and festivals, also on Mondays and Thursdays, a Cohen is the first called on to repeat the blessings. In Orthodox congregations he joins with the other Cohanim to bless the congregation, in the formula taken from the Book of Numbers: "The Lord bless thee and keep thee; the Lord make his spirit shine upon thee and be gracious unto thee; the Lord lift up his spirit unto thee and grant thee peace." These words are intoned with much solemnity, the Cohen raising his two hands over the heads of the congregants with thumbs and forefingers touching and the forefingers of each hand divided to form the letter "V." It is customary for the congregation not to gaze at the Cohanim during the moments of blessing.

In most American Orthodox congregations the blessing of the priests takes place only on the three major festivals. However I recently observed the ceremony on an ordinary Sabbath in the Grand Synagogue of Tel Aviv.

The Cohen also participates in the ceremony of Pidyon Haben (see p. 83). If, however, his own first-born is a son he need not observe this ritual of redemption.

A vestige of the original sanctity of the Cohanim remains in two restrictions still observed by the religious Cohen today: he may not enter within the gates of a cemetery except for the burial of his closest relatives; and he may not marry a divorced woman.

Related to the Cohanim are the Levites, those Jews who trace their ancestry to the Levites of biblical days. The duties of the levites were not priestly, but in the days of the ancient Temple they were responsible for the physical care of the sanctuary. The modern Levites (Levy, Levine, Levinson, Lewisohn and kindred names) retain the privilege of being called to the reading of the Torah immediately following the Cohen. And like the Cohen, Levites are also exempt from the Pidyon Haben ritual.

What Are the Most Important Prayers Which Jews Recite?

THE late Chief Rabbi of the British Empire, Joseph H. Hertz, whose commentaries on the Bible and the Prayer Book are, to my mind, the most illuminating Jewish works in the English language, described Jewish prayer as ranging from "half-articulate petition for help in distress to highest adoration, from confession of sin to jubilant expression of joyful fellowship with God, from thanksgiving to the solemn resolve to do His will as if it were our will."

Each of these prayers is found in the daily worship prescribed by Jewish tradition. Three times a day, the observant Jew repeats the Shema, watchword of Israel, in a pattern that has not been altered in twenty-five hundred years: "Hear O Israel, the Lord, our God, the Lord is One." At the same time, the worshiper recites from the Bible: "Thou shalt love the Lord thy God, with all thy heart, with all thy soul, and with all thy might."

A second core prayer is the Silent Devotion—eighteen benedictions—also repeated three times daily. Recited standing and without interruption, these devotions consist of three main thoughts: the glory of God; our hope for personal and group well-being; and our gratitude for God's blessings.

Concluding every worship service is the Adoration, which includes the universal prayer for the day when all men are united under the Kingdom of God.

Judaism has a prayer or blessing for almost every moment of the waking day. On rising we thank God for having "returned our souls, that were in His keeping, to us." There is a benediction for every one of life's bounties; even for the rather prosaic joy of eating fruit of various species the first time in the season. And at bedtime, we ask God to give us peace in our sleep: "Shelter us beneath the shadow of Thy wings. . . ." and "Let us not sleep the sleep of death."

A child's bedtime worship is somewhat simpler. After the Shema, the youngster prays: "Let me lie down in peace and rise again in peace. . . . Into Thy hand I place my spirit. . . ."

In ancient times, a recitation of the Ten Commandments was part of the daily worship. This custom was abandoned because the rabbis noted a tendency to enshrine the Ten Commandments almost as an object of worship, and because they felt people might think all of Judaism could be found in the Decalogue.

Much of our worship consists not in prayer, but in the recitation of the Psalms. In moments of trial and difficulty, the Psalms are read for comfort and strength. The 145th Psalm, which reflects our faith in God's benevolence, has been incorporated into morning, afternoon and evening worship: "The Lord is nigh to all who call upon Him; to all who call upon Him in sincerity. The Lord is good to all, and His tender compassion covers all His works."

Why Is a Quorum of Ten Men Needed for a Religious Service?

THE number ten apparently held a particular fascination for the Jews of antiquity. The Commandments were *ten* in number; Pharaoh was visited with ten plagues; the High Holy Days include *ten* Days of Penitence; *ten* generations are recorded between Adam and Noah and between Noah and Abraham; Abraham underwent *ten* tests of his faith, and so on. "God's presence," the rabbis declared, "rests upon any ten who gather in His name," and it was rabbinical law which established ten Jewish men as the minimum requirement for public worship. This quorum is known as a *minyan*.

This did not mean that private devotions are not acceptable. But certain community prayers are recited only in the presence of ten males over thirteen years of age. Other rituals also require the presence of a *minyan*: Marriage is a community affair (see p. 57) and must be celebrated in the presence of ten witnesses. The Kaddish (memorial prayer) is recited exclusively during public worship, for the mourner affirms his submission to God's will in the presence of his fellow men.

Reform Jews do not observe the requirement of the *minyan*. Any group of worshipers, few or many, male or female, may constitute themselves a congregation in a Reform synagogue.

What Is the Basis for the Dietary Laws Which Many Jews Still Obey?

JEWISH law based on the Book of Leviticus sets down certain definite dietary restrictions:

1. It is forbidden to eat the meat of certain animals, such as the pig and horse; and deep sea foods, such as shrimp, lobster, crab and oyster.

2. Meats must be slaughtered according to ritual and must meet specific health standards.

3. Meat products and dairy products may not be eaten together.

Food which is forbidden is *treyfah*, meaning unfit. The designation *kosher* indicates that the food which is permitted is *kosher*, meaning ritually correct. *Kosher* describes not only food, but any object which meets ritual requirements.

Those Jews who accept the laws of the Bible as everlastingly binding do not feel impelled to find "logical" explanations for observing these ancient dietary restrictions today. "We obey the laws of the Bible," they declare, "and we do not question them."

But for the past eight centuries, many serious-minded Jews have discussed the laws of Kashruth (those which define what is *kosher*) on rational grounds as well. Maimonides, a distinguished physician and philosopher of the twelfth century, considered Jewish food restrictions as a health measure—particularly in the case of pork, which deteriorated rapidly in the semitropical climate of Palestine. He also saw important moral values in applying restraint to our eating habits: If we can adhere to certain restraints in satisfying our appetite, it may help us to be more self-controlled in the face of other temptations.

Jewish ethics taught that the moral character consisted in resisting temptation. Thus, the ancient rabbis advised: "Do not say 'I do not like the meat of swine and therefore I reject it,' but rather 'I like it, but I do not eat it since the Torah forbids it to me.'"

The biblical injunction against having milk and meat at the same time is set down in the compassionate words, "Do not seethe the kid in its mother's milk." Another basis for the dietary restrictions lies in the strict injunction against inflicting pain on any living thing. Many of the laws concerning *kosher* food deal with the method of slaughtering the animal: it must be done without pain to the beast, with a steady hand, the greatest speed, the sharpest instruments and by a God-fearing person who has compassion for all God's creatures, who destroys life only with the greatest reluctance.

Originally, the word *treyfah* meant that the meat was procured by causing suffering to an animal. Even the meat of animals which cause pain to other beasts is forbidden; no carnivorous animals are *kosher*. Meat derived from the sport of hunting is also strictly taboo in Judaism. For we are forbidden to kill for the pleasure of the sport.

Jews who follow the dietary laws today feel no difficulty or sense of deprivation. They regard *kosher* practices as a symbol of their distinctive heritage, a daily lesson in self-discipline, and a constant reminder that a human being must feel pity for all living things.

Why Do Jews Practice Circumcision?

BRITH MILLAH—the circumcision of a male child a week after his birth—is the oldest rite in the Jewish religion. It was practiced by the patriarchs even before the laws of Moses existed and is so deeply ingrained in the tradition that no postponement is permitted either for the Sabbath or for the Day of Atonement. Only if the baby's health does not permit, can the ceremony be deferred.

Some scholars explain the requirement as a health measure, and modern medical science has lent support to this theory by advocating circumcision as a routine procedure in most maternity hospitals.

But Judaism considers the rite of circumcision an external symbol binding the child to his faith. It is not a sacrament which inducts the infant into Judaism: his birth does that. Circumcision confirms the child's status and represents a mark of loyalty to the faith of Israel.

Jewish law has set down a series of stringent requirements for the licensing of a *mohel*, who usually performs the circumcision operation. He must have the expert surgical skill needed for the task and he must be a God-fearing Jew. A *mohel* is not a rabbi, though he is sometimes referred to as such.

Some parents prefer that the circumcision be performed by

a Jewish surgeon. If the doctor fulfills the religious requirements and recites the appropriate blessings, the law is fulfilled. Some Reform and Conservative Jews invite a Jewish physician to perform the circumcision and a rabbi to read the ritual, but the Orthodox do not approve of this procedure.

The modern ceremony is quite impressive. The child is brought in by a godparent, and is greeted by the guests with the words, "Blessed be he who cometh." After the *mohel* has completed the circumcision and repeated a blessing, the father of the infant says: "Praised be Thou, O Lord our God, ruling Spirit of the Universe, who in sanctifying us with His commandments hath bidden us bring our son into the covenant of Abraham, our father."

The *mohel* or the rabbi then utters the prayer: "May the boy grow in vigor of mind and body to a love of Torah, to the marriage canopy, and to a life of good deeds."

Finally, a blessing over wine is made—and a drop placed on the infant's lips (possibly as a sedative). The child is then proudly borne out by another godparent, and the guests join in a happy celebration.

What Is Pidyon Haben?

PIDYON HABEN, the redemption of the first born, is a ceremonial rite observed by Orthodox and Conservative Jews when the first child born into a family is a boy.

This ritual, which takes place thirty days after the birth of the baby, is one of the oldest in the Hebrew tradition. It reaches far back to the dawn of Jewish history, when the first-born son was usually charged with the religious ritual of the household.

According to historic legend, the first-born of the Israelites were consecrated to God's service when the first-born of the Egyptians were smitten. But after the Exodus the duties of sanctuary worship were turned over to the Cohanim, the descendants of Aaron, and to the Levites, their assistants. The first-born were relieved of their ritual responsibilities, but theoretically, they had to acquire exemption by transferring their duties to one of the Cohanim.

The modern ceremony is a very brief and festive occasion in which friends and family all join. It takes the form of a little drama. The father holds the month-old infant in his arms and offers the Cohen, or priest (see p. 75), his choice of the child or five shekels (five silver dollars) for his son's redemption. The Cohen chooses the redemption money. (I recall the time when a gold coin was used, but since 1933, when the United States went off the gold standard, silver coins serve the purpose.)

The Cohen recites the formula of release, and pronounces the priestly benediction over the baby's head: "The Lord bless thee and keep thee . . .". Later, he makes a gift of the redemption sum to the infant.

If the father of the baby is a Cohen or Levite, or the mother a daughter of one, the family is exempted from the ritual.

Although Reform Judaism has abolished the custom, the Pidyon Haben has persisted in modern times. In fact, my own experience leads me to believe that the ceremony has grown in popularity, particularly since hospital restrictions have modified the elaborate festivities once connected with the circumcision rite.

It is interesting to note that despite his redemption, the first-born son is charged with one duty that remains with him throughout his life. Each year, on the eve of Passover, the first-born son of the Jewish family must fast—out of sympathy for the first-born among the Egyptians!

What Is Bar Mitzvah?

A BOY who reaches his thirteenth birthday is a Bar Mitzvah—literally a *man of duty*. From that day on, in Jewish tradition, he is responsible for his own deeds and for all the religious duties of a man.

On the Sabbath preceding the Jewish boy's thirteenth birthday, he is called to the altar of the synagogue to read the *Torah*. In the Orthodox and Conservative ritual, the young man repeats the blessing as a portion of the *Torah* is read and chants the lesson from the Prophets, called the *Haftarah*.

Measured in the broad span of Jewish history, the ceremony is of recent origin. Professor Theodore H. Gaster, well-known Jewish historian, tells us that it was unknown before the fourteenth century. Dr. Gaster also underscores the fact that "it is in no sense a sacramental rite." It simply marks the first time that a Jew, having reached the age of reason, exercises his right to participate fully in synagogue life, much as a citizen goes to the polls when he has passed his eighteenth birthday.

In many old European Jewish communities, it was customary for the Bar Mitzvah to deliver a scholarly discourse on the intricacies of talmudic law with which he was, by the age of thir-

teen, very familiar. It was not uncommon to hear as part of the
Bar Mitzvah address a thoughtful analysis of such themes as
civil and criminal courts, the problem of free will, or the laws
of marriage. Today, however, the Bar Mitzvah speech usually
consists of a solemn pledge by the boy to live up to the highest
ideals of his faith and to dedicate himself to the *Torah*. It is a
festive occasion for friends and family, with gifts to the young
man and a general air of celebration.

Over twenty years ago, some Conservative congregations in-
troduced a Bath Mitzvah ritual as a counterpart of the Bar
Mitzvah ceremony for girls reaching their thirteenth birthday.
Several Reform congregations have also adopted the custom.

Do Jews Have Confirmation Services?

IN THE nineteenth century Reform Judaism introduced the
group Confirmation service as a substitute for the individual
Bar Mitzvah ritual, extending this practice to girls as well as
boys as the first step in preparation for full membership in the
congregation.

Confirmation services are usually held for children of fifteen
or sixteen years of age, since it is felt that thirteen is too young
for modern youth to take on the responsibilities of adulthood.
In the early part of this century, the Confirmation ceremony
was held at various times of the year. But within the past two
decades the feast of Shevuoth, the day commemorating the Giving of the *Torah*, has been universally adopted by Reform congregations, and by many Conservative synagogues as well, as
the appropriate Confirmation date.

What Are T'fillin?

T'FILLIN, or phylacteries, consist of two small black boxes, one to two inches square, with leather straps attached. They contain four separate pieces of parchment inscribed with verses from the Books of Exodus and Deuteronomy proclaiming God's unity, His providential care, and Israel's deliverance from bondage.

The phylacteries are intended to remove the distractions of the mundane world and are worn, in a special way unchanged for centuries, by Orthodox and Conservative Jews during weekday morning prayers. One box is fastened to the left arm, the other is placed on the forehead. The intricacies of placing the *t'fillin* on arm and head according to prescribed ritual help to remove from the worshiper's mind any secular intrusions and help him concentrate on earnest devotions. On the Sabbath and festivals, when the usual weekday diversions are less present, phylacteries are not worn.

The symbolic purpose of phylacteries is to act as a reminder of man's closeness to God; to connote, as Rabbi Milton Steinberg once explained, our "commitment of heart and hand to God's will." The verses of the Bible placed on the left arm are near the heart, representing our emotional ties to our faith; the verses on the forehead, near the brain, represent our intellectual acceptance of God's truth.

What Is a Tallith and Why Do Jews Wear a Tallith at Prayer?

A TALLITH is a prayer shawl worn by Conservative and Orthodox Jews in obedience to an ancient biblical law. Though Reform Judaism has eliminated the use of the *Tallith* at general worship, some Reform rabbis wear it over their gowns while conducting worship or at a wedding ceremony.

The word *Tallith* means cloak and refers to a garment similar to the garb of the Arabs in the Near East or the robe of the ancient Romans. The *Tallith* of the Palestinian Jews, however, was distinguished by four fringes or tassels sewn at each of the robe's four corners, in fulfillment of the biblical injunction that every Jew must carry the fringes as a reminder of his faith.

Originally these fringes were both white and blue, but gradually the blue was eliminated because Jews in different lands could not find dyes to match the required shade. Blue and white have remained the colors of Judaism, and have been adopted by the new State of Israel.

The modern *Tallith*, made of silk or wool, is worn by male worshipers at all morning services (not at night, because in ancient times evening prayers were indoors, and the outer cloak was not worn). In the United States, most Jews use the silk prayer shawl, folded and worn as a scarf. The more pious prefer to wear it unfolded, so that it covers the shoulders and the back and the worshipers feel that they "take refuge in the shadow of His wings." During those portions of worship which call for complete concentration, they lift the shawl over their heads to eliminate any possible distraction.

A *Tallith* is usually given to the boy on the occasion of his Bar Mitzvah. Before his thirteenth birthday, he is not required to wear one at prayer. Some Orthodox congregations withhold the right to wear one until marriage.

Originally, the prayer shawl was a badge of distinction, worn only by scholars and elders. But today the *Tallith* is a mark of equality. All worshipers, regardless of their station in life, wear a similar garb. The *Tallith* may vary in texture and quality, but its general appearance and import is the same for all. And the pious Jew takes his *Tallith* with him to the grave, for it is part of his burial robe.

Do the Rabbi and Cantor Wear Special Vestments in Jewish Worship or at Other Times?

SPECIAL vestments are not a religious requirement for any worshiper. In most Conservative and Reform synagogues in America those who lead the services wear a black robe, a white prayer shawl, and, among the Conservative, an elaborate skull cap. Orthodox rabbis wear no special robes for prayer.

In Britain and on the continent, the vestments tend to be

more formal. Many English rabbis wear a clerical collar akin to
that of the Anglican clergy. In France the garb of the rabbi
bears a striking similarity to that of the Catholic priests. And I
have seen pictures of rabbis in Athens whose robes remind one
of the Greek Church.

American rabbis wear no distinctive clothing outside the synagogue. Officiating at a wedding in a home, for example, they
usually wear an ordinary business suit.

The long coats worn by some Orthodox rabbis are not a sign
of office. They are simply the garb of some pious Jews who
cling to the style of clothes worn by their forefathers of a century or two ago because for them that garb is a part of the tradition they cherish.

Do Jews Observe a Ritual of Grace at Meals?

WHENEVER observant Jews partake of food they "break
bread" with a benediction reminding them of their dependence
on God and on the labor of their fellow men. A second prayer
of grace is recited or chanted at the close of the meal. The Yiddish word for grace, *benschen*, is derived from the same Latin
root as the English word, benediction.

Traditionally, the dining hour in a Jewish home has always
been more than merely a time to satisfy hunger. The *Talmud*
spoke critically of those who sat through an entire dinner without exchanging "words of *Torah*." It was considered equivalent to practicing idolatry. But when words of wisdom and

learning passed across the table, God's spirit dwelt in the house. Thus, the meal took on the character of a sacrament.

The dominant theme of the mealtime benediction is thanksgiving. The family gives thanks to the Great Provider for "His loving kindness day after day," and humbly asks that they be worthy "in the sight of God and man." It is also a Jewish tradition that the doors of the home remain open at mealtime, so that the hungry stranger may enter and be fed. A vestige of this custom remains in the Passover Seder ritual (see p. 166), when the door is left ajar for the prophet Elijah, symbol of the lonely wayfarer.

On Sabbaths and festivals, when meals are eaten leisurely, grace is chanted rather than recited. The family first sings several "table hymns" and then chants Psalm 126: "They who sow in tears will reap in joy." The exact form of grace varies in every home but the central prayers are very ancient.

Above all, the mealtime atmosphere must be one of serenity and peace. An angry mood is taboo at the table and the melodies of grace are all happy and joyous.

Do All Jews Wear Hats When They Pray?

Most *Orthodox* Jews wear a hat or skull cap at all times—not only during prayer.

Conservative Jews cover the head only during acts of worship.

Reform Jews generally pray without hats.

Actually, as Professor Jacob Z. Lauterbach has pointed out, "The custom of praying bareheaded or with covered head is not at all a question of law. It is merely a matter of social propriety and decorum."

Like many old traditions, there has been a great deal of speculation about the origin of this practice. We know, of course, that the Jewish religion had its origin in the Near East. I have never encountered sunshine as bright and dazzling as I found in modern Jerusalem. Many centuries ago, too, Jews praying in the open court of the Temple of Jerusalem must have needed protection for their heads against the scorching sun.

Another explanation is that in ancient times Jews lifted their prayer shawls over their heads during worship to cover their eyes. This removed all distraction from prayer and made it possible to attain the greatest concentration. The hat or skull cap is the symbolic descendant of the prayer shawl covering.

We know from archeological remains that in ancient days, the people of Israel were often bareheaded. In the British Museum, I saw a bas-relief of the Assyrian king, Sennacherib, portraying Jews who wore no headgear. The modern Orthodox practice, therefore, of keeping the head covered at all times does not go back to ancient Palestine.

However, in the East the privileged classes wore some head ornament as a sign of their status and in time this custom spread to all groups. The early Europeans, who always went bareheaded, also borrowed the custom of wearing headgear from the Near East.

There is a tendency by all faiths to exalt customs into firmly established religious principle. So the head covering, originally a symbol of aristocracy, became the symbol of respect and reverence.

Extremely Orthodox Jewish women wear a wig as a mark of

piety. This custom has a curious history. In ancient times Jewish women were forbidden to expose their hair. Only the most immodest women would defy this convention.

In talmudic times, however, the custom of wearing a wig evidently fell into disuse. But in the eighteenth century, women again began to wear wigs, this time in imitation of the courts of Paris and Vienna. The rabbis were shocked by this daring circumvention of Jewish law. For the wig prescribed by ancient law was not meant as an adornment, to attract attention, but rather as a way of covering up attractive appearance in order to avoid attention. To copy the frivolities of French nobility was deemed, by the eighteenth-century rabbis, as little short of scandalous. But fashion prevailed in spite of rabbinical protests. The practice was soon widespread—and was handed down as a religious rite long after the styles in headdress changed. The granddaughters of these defiant women came to regard their grandmothers' wigs as symbols of their piety. And symbols of piety they remain!

Is There a Prohibition Against Shaving in Judaism?

THE origin of the ban against shaving is clearly stated in a biblical law found in the Book of Leviticus. The tonsure worn by some of the neighbors of the Israelites was part of a pagan ritual, and shaving one's head in a manner which imitated this pagan rite was strictly forbidden.

When Jews were dispersed throughout the world, they continued the practice of letting the beard grow. In some of the Mediterranean countries, where the beard was an exception, they found the custom awkward, and followed local usage. But until the late nineteenth century, in many countries including the United States, a clean-shaven face was the exception, and the biblical law was preserved without difficulty.

A beard is still sentimentally regarded as a mark of piety among many observant Jews. The patriarchs, the prophets, the ancient rabbis were all bearded, and there is therefore an inclination to associate a beard with dignity and mature judgment. Jewish literature is full of references to the beauty of a fine bearded face.

Today, the majority of Jews in most countries have given up the beard. The very Orthodox will not use a razor, but scissors, depilatories, or electric razors, are used.

There seems little doubt that the biblical law, which was directed against a specific form of pagan observance, has been largely reinterpreted out of existence.

What Is the Meaning of the Various Death Rituals in the Jewish Religion?

IT IS only natural that a religious group with a continuous tradition of scores of centuries would create a pattern of ceremonial surrounding man's greatest crisis—the end of his life. These customs have grown out of community experiences and group values. Some are vestiges of primitive superstition. Others, despite Judaism's determination to avoid "alien practices," were borrowed from the people among whom the Jews lived.

Jewish families have for generations observed a fixed pattern of mourning when death struck. According to Orthodox tradition, burial must take place without delay; only if a Sabbath or holy day intervenes may the body remain unburied for longer than twenty-four hours. This rule has been somewhat relaxed in Conservative or Reform practice, but lengthy wakes, or having the deceased "lie in state" for any length of time is completely foreign to Judaism.

The funeral arrangements must be as simple as possible. Jewish law forbids elaborate funerals, on the principle that all men are equal in death. Since the first century, the custom of Rabbi Gamaliel has been followed: the shroud consists of a simple linen vestment; the coffin must be of plain wood, without adornment of any kind. The ancient rabbis insisted on this "democracy in death," so that no poor family would be embarrassed or forced into excessive expenditures because of the ostentatious funerals of their wealthy neighbors.

At Orthodox Jewish funerals flowers are not permitted and music may not be played, since they are both considered symbols of joy inappropriate in mourning.

Cremation of the dead is also alien to Jewish tradition. For though Judaism stresses that our souls are more important than our bodies, our tradition frowns upon the deliberate destruction of "man made in the image of God." On the other hand, a Reform Guide permits cremation, suggesting that "the ashes be buried in a Jewish cemetery."

After the funeral services, the first period of mourning is called Shiva (literally seven: the seven days of mourning). Actually, there are only six or even fewer days. Mourning is forbidden on the Sabbath. If a religious festival falls during this period of mourning, Shiva is not resumed after the holiday.

The obligation to "sit Shiva" is limited to the immediate next-of-kin: the children, parents, brothers and sisters and mate of the deceased. They may not leave their home, except for Sabbath worship. A special home service is conducted three times a day, at which the next-of-kin repeat the Kaddish. (In earlier days only men were required to recite Kaddish. Today in most services Kaddish is recited by both sexes.)

The Kaddish prayer is the most distinctive feature of the Jewish observance of mourning. Its words are Aramaic, not Hebrew, and it contains no direct reference to death or the dead. Beginning with the words, "Magnified and sanctified is the name of the Lord," it is simply an affirmation of faith in the wisdom of God's decrees.

During the week of Shiva it is customary for neighbors to visit the family, offering whatever consolation and practical help they can. One of the greatest *mitzvahs*, or good deeds, a Jew can perform, is to bring the first meal to his sorrowing neighbor. The *Talmud* suggests that the food be brought in wicker baskets, again to prevent competition among the neighbors who might be tempted to outdo others.

After the first week, a general period of mourning continues for eleven months, during which the Kaddish is repeated daily (some mourners continue the practice only on Sabbaths). Before the first anniversary a memorial stone is unveiled at the graveside.

After the first year, a special memorial prayer, Yizkor, is recited in the synagogue on the Day of Atonement and on the last days of Passover, Succoth and Shevuoth by those who have lost parents, children, brothers or sisters, and husbands or wives.

Annually on the anniversary of the death, Yahrzeit, the family also recites a prayer and lights a candle in honor of the deceased. This is a ritual clearly borrowed, centuries ago, from the non-Jewish community in which the Jews lived. It is, in fact, the only Jewish ritual which has no Hebrew name. The historian, Israel Abrahams, suggests that the original observance might be traced to the Persians, and that the custom of candle-lighting was adopted by the early Catholic church. In Germany the term Jahrzeit was used in the church to describe masses in memory of the dead. In any case, Orthodox Jews observe Yahrzeit today, unaware (or unmindful) of its non-Jewish birth.

In addition to these religious rituals there are several Jewish mourning customs which are pure superstition—and which are more or less on the wane among modern Jews. It was customary, for example, to cover all the mirrors in a house of mourning—a practice stemming from an ancient fear that the spirit of the dead might be confused by his own image and remain in the house. Upon leaving the cemetery the members of the funeral procession would wash their hands and toss a twig over their shoulders—clearly a remnant of old magical thinking. And in most Orthodox services, even today, non-mourners leave the synagogue during Yizkor not in adherence to any religious law, but in conformity with the ancient notion that mourning might be catching.

For the most part these practices were discouraged by rabbinical authorities, but custom proved stronger than reason. All the mourning rituals, however, serve the same purpose: they strengthen family solidarity, and they impress upon the bereaved the message of the funeral liturgy, "to number our days that we may get us a heart of wisdom."

Do Jews Have a Confessional, Deathbed or Otherwise?

YES, there is a confessional, a collective one recited by all Jews annually on the Day of Atonement. The Orthodox Jew also recites a daily confessional as part of his daily prayers. Individual confessions, however, are made only twice in a lifetime: immediately before the marriage ceremony and in the closing moments on earth.

The Jewish confessional is an outpouring of the heart directly to God—without human mediation. A witness is present at the deathbed act of contrition, but he need not be a rabbi. No one, be he a rabbi or any other dignitary, has the power to transmit God's absolution.

Confession of sin to a sympathetic pastor obviously has much psychological value, and many rabbis receive such confidences from their congregants. But our tradition does not consider it an instrument of atonement, or of reconciling the confessant to God.

If the sin was committed against another human being, only restitution and begging forgiveness of the one aggrieved can effect atonement. A sin against God can be forgiven only through sincere repentance, an honest resolve to avoid repetition of the transgression in the future.

Maimonides pointed out that God does not need the confession, but the sinner needs it to know himself better.

The deathbed formula of confession (written seven hundred years ago), begins with a prayer for healing, and continues with these words: ". . . but if my death be fully determined by Thee, I will accept it in love from Thy hand. May my death be an atonement for all my iniquities against Thee. . . . Make known to me the path of life, for in Thy presence is the fullness of joy. . . . O Father of the fatherless, protect my beloved kinfolk with whose souls my own is knit. Into Thy hand I commend my spirit. . . . Amen, amen!" Then follows the affirmation of Israel: "The Lord is God . . . Hear O Israel, the Lord our God, the Lord is One."

How Can Friends Appropriately Extend Comfort to a Jewish Family in Mourning?

FUNERAL notices involving a Jewish family frequently include the request: "Please omit flowers." While this restriction is far less rigidly observed today than in the past, it is generally wise to respect the tradition. "A meal of the comforters," prepared by friends of the mourners, is prescribed by Jewish law. To some, this may suggest a home-cooked dinner; others may bring a basket of food, fruit or candy.

"An act of kindness redeems man from death," said an ancient tradition. In this spirit friends sometimes decide on a contribution to a worthwhile cause as a meaningful tribute.

Always, of course, a personal letter or a simple condolence card is an appropriate note of comfort to the bereaved.

Is Excommunication Practiced in Judaism?

THE Hebrew term for "excommunication" is *herem*, which is a linguistic cousin of the Arabic word harem. The two words have a very similar connotation. In the Jewish tradition, excommunication meant the setting apart of individuals guilty of crimes or breaches of Jewish law.

In the Middle Ages, the Jews of the ghetto were granted a considerable amount of autonomy and self-government. Matters which involved a Jew and non-Jews outside the ghetto were decided in the courts of the feudal lord or other local nobleman. But within the ghetto, both civil and religious transgressions were left to the rabbis to deal with. Rabbinical courts, or courts of community elders, were established to handle offenses of all kinds, and excommunication, or banishment from the social and religious life of the community was one of the major punishments meted out.

As in modern systems of punishment, this penalty was imposed for widely varying periods of time, depending on the gravity of the offense. The term of the sentence could be a day, a month, a year, or even, in some rare instances, a lifetime.

Morris S. Goodblatt, in his study *Jewish Life in Turkey*, describes an excommunication ruling in an account of a sixteenth-century trial involving a man who had maligned another man's wife. The lady in question was the local rabbi's daughter, and the rabbi prevailed upon the community council to invoke the following penalties against the offender: (a) that he be publicly excommunicated; (b) that he be compelled to move some distance from his present home which was near the woman he had slandered; (c) that he not be counted in a *minyan* (quorum of worshipers); (d) that he be ineligible for public office; (e) that he be required to change his permanent synagogue pew; (f) that he be ineligible to be called to the reading of the *Torah*.

These penalties were so severe than an appeal was made to a higher court, which consisted of a rabbi whose moral authority was widely accepted. The latter summarily reversed the decision and decided that all that should be required of the defendant was a public apology.

This example is cited to explain that excommunication was most often a punishment for a *civil* or *social* offense, and almost never for a transgression of religious dogma. There were, however, certain notable exceptions to this in periods when the heresy hunts of the medieval world cast their benighted influence on the Jewish world as well.

In Amsterdam in the seventeenth century, the Jewish community was so intolerant of any deviation from orthodox teachings, that when Uriel da Costa wrote a treatise against the narrow ritualism into which Judaism had degenerated, he was accorded much the same treatment which Galileo endured for his beliefs. Da Costa was forced to participate in a ceremony of excommunication during which each member of the congregation stepped over his prostrate form on the threshold of the synagogue. Shortly afterward, he took his life. The philosopher Baruch Spinoza came under a similar ban for his advanced and highly unorthodox writings. But unlike da Costa,

Spinoza was quite willing to withdraw from the community into his own world of books and speculation.

These lapses into bigotry are fortunately rare in the long history of Judaism. Abram L. Sachar, noted contemporary historian, refers to that era as "the age of degeneration," and declares, "The tragedy would not have been possible if the demoralization of Jewish life had not driven its leaders into a fearful and *thoroughly un-Jewish* intolerance."

Excommunication is virtually unknown in modern Judaism. Its effectiveness lay in the compactness of Jewish community life in the past and in the moral authority conferred by the community on some outstanding rabbis. Today, few people would abide by such sanctions; but more important, no recognized rabbi would assume so broad a mantle of authority.

Is There a Central State, Regional or National Authority in Judaism?

IN SOME European countries, a central Jewish religious authority is recognized, but in no case does it cross national boundaries. The United Synagogue of Great Britain, for example, appoints a Chief Rabbi of the country and maintains strict control in matters of marriage and divorce.

The Israel Chief Rabbinate is also granted authority in all matters relating to marital status in that country.

The Jewish Consistoire in France is a central religious authority and the official voice of French Jewry, but its power rests in lay rather than clerical hands. In July, 1952, when I attended the funeral of the Chief Rabbi of France in Paris, I noted that the service was directed by the lay leadership of the Consistoire, and the ritual portion assigned to the rabbinate.

In the United States, there is no central Jewish authority, either religious or communal. Each synagogue is completely autonomous; a congregation affiliated with one branch of Judaism may, whenever it so decides, join another wing. The rabbi of each synagogue is selected by a vote of its membership, and is not assigned to it by any national body.

There is no equivalent of a bishop in the American Jewish community. No rabbi is empowered to determine the status of a colleague, or to place him in a pulpit.

Nor are there any regional or state authorities. Even the New York Board of Rabbis, with a membership of over six hundred Orthodox, Conservative and Reform rabbis, has no directive powers. The Board helps develop standards for Jewish religious life, and uses its moral influence in civic and synagogue affairs, but it is a purely voluntary body, whose influence is based solely on the respect and esteem in which it is held.

Each of the three branches of Judaism, Orthodox, Conservative and Reform, has two national bodies, one consisting of rabbis and the other of laymen. The Union of Orthodox Jewish Congregations (lay) and the Rabbinical Council of America are both Orthodox. The United Synagogue of America (lay) and the Rabbinical Assembly of America are the two Conservative groups. The Union of American Hebrew Congregations (lay) and the Central Conference of American Rabbis are both Reform.

All of these are *voluntary* associations of lay people and spiritual leaders who have joined together to share experiences, develop standards and engage in various united religious and community activities.

The discipline which American Jewish congregations accept

is self-imposed. Their national bodies do not interfere with the internal affairs of the synagogue in matters of worship, administration, structure or the selection of a specific rabbi. The influence of these parent bodies is purely moral: they may urge standards of ritual worship, but they cannot compel conformity. This explains the wide diversity within the three groups (see p. 118).

The rabbinical bodies have the right to expel members from their own ranks, but only the theological seminary grants the rabbinical degree and has the power to withdraw a rabbi's ordination. From a practical point of view such discipline rarely if ever is exercised.

American Jewish religious life has several other distinctive features. Religious activities are not, as in other lands, exclusively under synagogue control. The religious life of Jewish college students is served by the B'nai B'rith Hillel Foundations, a lay organization. The National Jewish Welfare Board, another lay body, ministers to the spiritual needs of Jewish men and women in the Armed Services. Though rabbis cooperate with both groups, neither is under rabbinical control.

An American Jew is also completely free to select that branch of Judaism which he prefers. Unlike British Jewry, whose official national synagogue is Orthodox, or French Jewry, whose official religious authority is liberal Orthodox, the three American groups, Orthodox, Conservative and Reform, all enjoy equal status. The Synagogue Council of America, a coordinating organization of the three groups, selects officials from all three branches. And the very existence of this range of religious expression precludes any central authority for American Jews.

V

CUSTOMS AND TRADITIONS

Do you know where the Lord is to be found? He is in the place where He is invited to enter.

HASIDIC SAYING

Customs and Traditions

It is not easy to draw any rigid lines separating Jewish law and Jewish custom. There is an ancient saying that in Judaism custom becomes law. And the history of Judaism will reveal many religious laws later widely recognized and observed, which had their origin in long-accepted folk practices.

Dr. Solomon Schechter, founder of Conservative Judaism, described this phenomenon with the curious phrase "catholic Israel" (catholic in the sense of universal). When the vast majority of *observant* Jews adopted a certain way of practicing a ritual—or chose to disregard it—the custom ultimately became law.

This is not a new or a modern innovation. In any standard manual of Jewish law, we often find such introductory comments as: "This is the practice among Italian Jews; the French follow another custom," or "Among the Spanish Jews, there is a tendency to be lenient in this matter; German Jews are more stringent . . ." No authority suggests that there is a single unalterable form of practice, or, for that matter, a single prayer book to be followed by all Jews.

Another factor which complicates our understanding of Jewish traditions and customs is the manner in which superstitions and local non-Jewish practices were adopted by the Jews and interwoven with the various religious rites which they observed.

Judaism was born out of mankind's revolt against primitive superstition and witchcraft. It was Abraham, father of the Jewish religion, who smashed the pagan idols in his father's sculpture shop and first proclaimed the existence of One God, Father to all living things.

The image of the child Abraham with axe in hand symbolizes Judaism's rejection of magical thinking—a rejection which is stressed in all the laws and commentary of the Jewish religion.

The Bible tells us, however, that it was not easy for the followers of Abraham to root out all the superstitions of the past or to remain completely aloof from the beliefs and practices of their neighbors. Thus, Moses came down from Sinai to find Jews worshiping the golden calf, and Jewish leaders have often, through the years, had to do similar battle against the inroads of ignorance and false belief.

Today, though idolatry and other gross superstitions of that nature are long of the past, there still remain in Jewish custom and tradition certain practices whose origins can be traced to primitive, superstitious beliefs.

Some of these are really folk customs and have nothing whatsoever to do with religious observance. These include the automatic *Gesundheit* or *Zu Gesundt* (to your health) told to someone who sneezes—a custom widely practiced by almost every faith and nationality; and the many phrases like *kein ayin horoh, unbeschrien, unberufen*, all meaning "may no evil spirit befall," which are so often used when speaking of good health or personal success.

There are also superstitious origins in certain commonly accepted religious practices which have no actual basis in Jewish law. Among these is the taboo against naming children after living relatives (see p. 61); the ban against double marriages of two brothers or two sisters (because too much happiness would tempt envious spirits); the Old World custom of guarding a newborn child against evil by hanging a charm necklace with the 127th Psalm, or other significant phrases from the Scriptures, around its neck. Such customs have remained deeply ingrained in Orthodox Jewish life despite the opposition of the rabbis through the ages. They are only now being discarded in modern Jewish homes.

Finally, there are those superstitious practices, adopted by some Jews from the surrounding culture, which are actually completely alien to our tradition, such as knocking on wood for good luck or crossing one's fingers. Since both of these customs most likely refer back to the wooden crucifix of Christianity and the sign of the cross, they obviously have no precedent in Jewish life. Jewish tradition also frowns on the custom of wearing black as a sign of mourning—a practice which harks back to the Near Eastern peoples, who usually wore white clothing and put on dark clothes to hide their identity from the death messenger.

On the other hand, throwing rice and confetti at weddings, which can be traced back to an ancient fertility rite, is a custom frequently found at Jewish weddings, and is neither blessed nor banned by Jewish law.

Of course, not all informal customs have their origin in primitive belief. Many folkways, colorful and meaningful, have their origin in Jewish doctrine.

The pliability of Judaism has always permitted a great range *within* the traditional fold. The Jewish religion has never been a fertile breeding ground for separate sects and denominations. It did not suppress opposition—it simply absorbed it.

A person who chose to follow the mystics or the Hasidim merely exercised his right to use his personal preference on what was important among the elements of his faith. Often there was ill feeling between the followers of Hasidism and their opponents, but no one thought of ruling his fellow Jew to be outside the mainstream of tradition.

Thus no common word for sect or denomination exists in Hebrew, and even in the English language we are hard put to find a word expressive of the at-one-time differences and similarities in Orthodox, Conservative and Reform.

A serious student of the Jewish religion will try to distinguish between the generally accepted law, the widely accepted practice and the variety of popular superstitions and folkways not indigenous to Judaism. But to the extent that they affect and influence the pattern of Jewish life, all three are inseparable ingredients of Judaism's customs and traditions.

Why Does the Jewish Day Begin at Sunset?

THE custom of reckoning the day from sunset to sunset is based on the story of Creation as depicted in Genesis: "It was evening, it was morning, the first day." The evening came first! Thus, each new day begins with the sunset of the one before. The Sabbath is ushered in as the sun sets on Friday. And if the Feast of Purim falls on March 15th, the celebration actually begins on the evening of the 14th.

During the period of the First Commonwealth (prior to 586

B.C.E.) the day was not reckoned in terms of hours. In fact, the word "hour" is not found anywhere in the Bible, even as a figure of speech. The night was divided into three watches, the early watch, the middle watch and the morning watch. (Hence such biblical sayings as "Watchman, what of the night?") The day was divided into forenoon and afternoon.

When the Jews returned to Palestine after their Babylonian exile (516 B.C.E.) they brought back with them the Babylonian astronomy and way of reckoning time. But they still clung to a rather curious way of dividing the daylight hours: an hour was a twelfth part of daylight—longer in summer than in winter. Apparently they had much less of a passion for uniformity than modern man.

This lack of exactitude is still followed with regard to Sabbaths, festivals and fasts, for Jewish tradition stretches the day a little: a few minutes is added at either end—and even an hour or two among the more observant. It is considered unseemly to begin the Sabbath or other holy day at the last moment, or to end it at the earliest opportunity. During the High Holy Day season, after the Feast of Tabernacles, an entire day has been added in keeping with this custom. The day is called Shemini Atzereth, the Eighth Day of Assembly, and has no historic significance whatever, though it is observed as zealously as other holidays. Folklore offers the following explanation: The Almighty, who has been close to the children of Israel during this season of the year, says: "It is too hard for Me to take leave of you—let Me linger yet another day!"

An ordinary day, therefore, is calculated in the Jewish tradition from the moment of sunset to the next moment of sunset. The day consists of *exactly* twenty-four hours only twice a year, during the equinoxes, and at other times is a few minutes longer or shorter, depending on the season.

As for the Sabbath, the Day of Atonement and other meaningful days in the Jewish calendar—they are generally closer to twenty-five hours. Mathematical precision yields to the needs of the spirit.

What Is the Torah?

THE word *Torah* has two usages in Jewish tradition. Broadly, *Torah* is our way of life, or, as Milton Steinberg expressed it, "All the vastness and variety of the Jewish tradition." It is synonymous with learning, wisdom, love of God. Without it, life has neither meaning nor value.

More narrowly, the *Torah* is the most revered and sacred *object* of Jewish ritual—the beautiful, hand-written scroll of the Five Books of Moses (the Bible from Genesis to Deuteronomy) which is housed in the Ark of the Synagogue.

The *Torah* scroll is made of parchment, wrapped around two wooden poles or rollers. It is covered with an embroidered cloth. Silver ornaments rest on the poles and a silver breastplate adorns the covering. The text of the *Torah*, drafted in a Hebrew unchanged through countless generations, must be letter-perfect. A *Torah* containing two scribal errors may not be used in worship.

A portion of the *Torah*, starting with the book of Genesis, is read aloud every Sabbath during worship, beginning right after the High Holy Days and continuing each week until the entire *Torah* has been read by the end of the Jewish year. The worshiper stands when the *Torah* is taken out of the Ark. A pious Jew kisses the *Torah* by placing his prayer shawl on the parchment (so his fingers will not touch the scroll) and then lifting the fringes of the shawl to his lips.

In Jewish folklore, the *Torah* is supposed to antedate the time of Creation. It was at the Creator's side when the world came into being. To the observant Jew, the *Torah* is the very breath of life. Men have bled and died to save this sacred scroll from desecration. Throughout history, Jews who were forced to flee their homes in the face of tyranny and persecution abandoned all their worldly goods but carried the *Torah* with them into the unknown.

What Is the Talmud?

THE *Talmud* consists of sixty-three books of legal, ethical and historical writings of the ancient rabbis. It was edited in the year 499 c.e. in the religious academies of Babylonia, where most Jews of that period lived.

The *Talmud* is a compendium of law and lore, and has been for centuries the major textbook of Jewish schools. Knowledge of its contents is, even today, the most important training of Orthodox and Conservative rabbis. Orthodox Jewish law is based largely on the decisions found in the *Talmud*.

A considerable portion of this encyclopedic work is of interest only to well-informed students of law. But the *Talmud* is much more than a series of legal treatises. Interlaced with the discussions of the scholars are thousands of parables, biographical sketches, humorous anecdotes and epigrams that provide an intimate glimpse into Jewish life in the days just before and after the destruction of the Jewish state. It is a storehouse of wisdom as real today as it was eighteen hundred years ago.

Many of the moral maxims of the *Talmud* have become household phrases: "Give every man the benefit of the doubt." "An ignorant man cannot be a pious man." "Don't look at the flask but what it contains." "One good deed invariably leads to another; an evil deed always brings another in its wake."

The rabbis possessed remarkable insight into the minds of children. "Do not threaten a child. Either punish him or forgive him." The *Talmud* also has much to say about education: "A classroom should never have more than twenty-five pupils." "When you encounter a child whose head is as solid as iron, you may be sure that his teacher did not have a pleasant way of explaining things." "Always begin the lesson with a humorous illustration."

One of the rabbinic teachers classified his students into four categories: "The *sponge*: he absorbs and retains everything; the *funnel*: everything that goes in comes out; the *sifter*: he remembers the trivial and forgets the significant; the *sieve*: he retains the important and sifts out the incidental."

Another scholar told his students: "He who does not study deserves to die!" Still another summed up his education: "Much have I learned from my teachers; even more from my classmates; but most of all, from my students!"

The rabbis were fond of pithy sayings: "Bad neighbors count a man's income but not his expenses." Or cryptic ones: "Better a tail to lions than a head to foxes."

Occasionally their words were half in jest: "Judge a man not according to the words of his mother, but according to the comments of his neighbors."

Profound truths, moral insights and spiritual values were stressed in homey examples from the lives of the rabbis. Rabbi

Jose overheard his wife reproving a maid unjustly. "Why blame the maid if you are not absolutely certain?" he asked. Later his wife complained: "Even if I'm wrong, you shouldn't have criticized me in the maid's presence." "Quite to the contrary," Rabbi Jose rejoined, "she ought to know that her rights are not denied."

The parables of the *Talmud* are familiar favorites in Jewish religious school literature. Rabbi Meir and Rabbi Akiba are as well known to the children as the biblical Jacob and Esau. Every child is taught the story of Honi, the traveler, who met a very, very old man busily planting a carob tree. "When will you be able to eat the fruit of the tree?" asked Honi. "In seventy years," replied the old man. "Do you expect to live that long?" the traveler queried. "I did not find the world desolate when I entered it," was the reply. "So I plant for those who come after me."

A particular talmudic favorite of mine is the thought-provoking comment: "Why is it that we are born into the world with clenched fists and leave it with outstretched fingers? To remind us that we take nothing with us."

The same wise rabbis who gave us the *Talmud* also compiled the *Midrash*, a collection of rabbinical commentary on the moral teachings of the Bible, frequently quoted in sermons and Jewish literature. Around each verse of the Scriptures the scholars wove some significant moral thought, often in the form of a parable or an illustration from life. The rabbis studied the Bible with the conviction that all truth was locked in its pages. One had merely to keep looking to unseal its great store of wisdom.

The aphorisms of the *Midrash*, like those of the *Talmud*, have become part of the language not only of Israel, but of all mankind. Many of the "sayings of the rabbis" quoted in these pages are taken from that source.

"All is well that ends well" is at least as old as the *Midrash*. Or, "Offer not pearls to those who deal in vegetables and onions."

"When in a city—follow its customs,"—the Jewish expression for "When in Rome . . ."

But these brief insights into life and people are only a small portion of the wisdom of the *Midrash*. Another telling example is the answer given the students of the *Torah* when they asked why God handed down the Law in the wilderness, rather than in some important city. "So that no nation could lay exclusive claim to its teachings," decided the rabbis. "So that all people who followed its precepts would share equal possession of the Law."

Is There a Universal Language Among Jews?

IF AN international conference were called today, bringing together Jews of a dozen different countries, no single language would be understood by all.

This fact is a source of wonder to many Jews and non-Jews alike. During World War II, I was stationed in Italy, France and North Africa, and I frequently saw a look of amazement on the faces of American Jewish soldiers who addressed the elders of a synagogue in Yiddish and found no response. In Dijon, most Jews were at home only with their native French; in Algiers, Arabic and French were the languages in most Jewish homes; and in Naples, only a rare soul had ever heard a word of Yiddish.

Hebrew, the language of prayer and the Bible, is spoken only by Israelis and a handful of scholars, though the rebirth of Israel has done a great deal to revive Hebrew as a spoken language.

Yiddish, a mixture of early German and Hebrew, is today unintelligible to Jews of Italy, Turkey, Spain, North Africa, a goodly number of Americans, and many native-born Israelis.

Ladino, a folk tongue of the Sephardic Jews of the Mediterranean, is also understood by very few.

A generation ago the vast majority of Jews in the western world could read and write Yiddish. It was, and in some measure still is, the most common medium of Jewish literary expression. Great works of poetry, drama and fiction are to be found in Yiddish. The whimsical writings of Sholom Aleichem, the artistic prose of I. L. Peretz and the creations of a score of contemporary writers are read and appreciated by a large number of Jews and, in translation, by non-Jews as well. In Latin America, Yiddish is universally understood and studied in the Jewish communities.

The nearest approach to a universal Jewish language since the destruction of the ancient state, was Aramaic. It was the spoken language of Babylonian Jewry, the largest single Jewish settlement. Much of the *Talmud* was written in Aramaic. One of the most sacred Jewish prayers, the Kaddish, (see p. 96) was never translated from the Aramaic into Hebrew. Because this was, for a long time, the language of the scholars, subsequent generations invested Aramaic with an aura of sanctity. It became a kind of holy tongue, with which no one dared to tamper.

To some degree this experience has been repeated with Yiddish. Many Orthodox seminaries in the western world today insist that Yiddish be the language of instruction, especially in

the study of the *Talmud*, because this is the way it has been
studied in those schools for centuries.

But just as the Jews of Babylonia adopted Aramaic and all
but lost Hebrew as a spoken tongue, Jews throughout the
world today have as their first, and most often their only, language the tongue of the land in which they live.

Are There Various Creeds and Sects Among Jews?

IN AMERICAN Judaism there are basically three religious
groupings: the Orthodox, the Conservative and the Reform
(sometimes called the Liberal). It would be inaccurate to designate them as sects or denominations, because that would imply
sharper differences than really exist. Actually, many Jews are
members in good standing of different synagogues representing two or even all three branches of Judaism. Also the home
practices of some Jews may be Conservative while their ritual
standards outside the home may follow the Reform pattern.
The lines are often blurred even within an individual family.
One brother may be a pillar of the Orthodox synagogue, another a leader in Conservative Judaism, and a third an active
member of a Reform congregation.

The *Orthodox* Jew looks upon his faith as the mainstream of
a tradition that has been steadfast and unaltered for the past
three thousand years. He accepts biblical law as the revealed
will of God, and believes with equal fervor in what he calls the
Oral Law—the traditional interpretations of the Mosaic Law as

embodied in the *Talmud* and other legal codes. His way of life does not change with each new "wind of doctrine"; it yields, he explains, neither to expediency nor to comfort.

Orthodox Jews are the strictest observers of the Sabbath (no work of any kind, no travel, writing or business dealings, no carrying of money, not even a discussion of weekday affairs). They adhere to every detail of the dietary laws; they maintain separate pews for women in the synagogue; and they use only Hebrew in prayer and ceremonial services.

Orthodox men and women both wear a head covering at all times. Men may not use a razor for shaving, though a depilatory is permitted.

Orthodox children receive religious instruction daily after public school, or in all-day schools which combine secular and Jewish studies (see p. 32).

Orthodox Jews pray three times daily: in the morning, at late afternoon, and after sunset. The exact time is not fixed by the clock, but by the sun. Thus evening services may be held as early as 4:30 P.M. in December, and as late as 9 P.M. in July.

Orthodoxy is not completely unbending to the contingencies in life. Although it is forbidden to eat on the Day of Atonement, for example, it is also forbidden to fast on that day if not eating endangers life.

Orthodox Jews in military service are also permitted some latitude in dietary observance.

Reform or Liberal Judaism differs sharply with Orthodoxy on the matter of Revelation. A Reform Jew accepts as binding only the *moral* laws of the Bible, and those ceremonies that "elevate and sanctify our lives." He does not abide by those customs that "are not adapted to the views and habits of modern civilization."

Reform Jews feel that faith must be rational and capable of

withstanding the careful scrutiny of reason and science. As a result, Reform worship departs from traditional forms. There is complete equality between the sexes in the temple. Prayer is largely in English (or any vernacular); there is a greater flexibility in the choice of prayers; instrumental music is permitted in the synagogue; and male worshipers do not wear the prayer shawl or *tallith*. Reform worship is conducted by the rabbi, with a cantor, choir or laymen as assistants. The Reform house of worship is called either a synagogue or temple; its architecture varies little from the Orthodox, except for the introduction of some technical changes (public address systems may not be used on the Sabbath in an Orthodox synagogue).

Conservative Jews follow the pattern of traditional Judaism, by and large, but unlike their Orthodox coreligionists, they believe that "Jewish law, like every other living manifestation, must necessarily grow if it is to remain alive," and they feel that change should be the result of natural growth and in consonance with the spirit of Jewish law. They regard Reform Judaism as too sharp a break with the past.

The Conservative Jew adheres to the dietary laws, with only minor relaxation, and observes the Sabbath, High Holy Days and festivals traditionally. On the other hand, he has borrowed many of the forms of Reform Judaism, such as the late Friday evening service, responsive readings, fixed hours of worship, and a more extensive use of English in prayers.

Although these represent the basic differences between Orthodox, Reform and Conservative Jews, there is a wide range of diversity within all three groups, for there is no element of compulsion in the American synagogue.

Some Orthodox groups are a replica of those found in Eastern Europe a century ago. At the other extreme are synagogues which are not too strict in the matter of separate pews, which permit some English prayers to be read, and which use Reform textbooks in their religious schools.

Conservative Judaism declares, in the words of Dr. Mordecai M. Kaplan, that its very strength lies in "unity in diversity." At one end of the spectrum are forms of worship virtually indistinguishable from Orthodoxy, and at the other, such innovations as experimentation with new prayer books, the use of organ music, and the Bath Mitzvah ritual (see p. 86).

Reform Judaism, too, is far from uniform: some congregations pray with covered heads, and others, of the extreme liberal wing, have services on Sunday instead of Saturday.

In addition to these three religious groupings, a movement called *Reconstructionism* has won a considerable following in American Jewish life. Founded by Dr. Kaplan, Reconstructionism has its supporters among Conservative and Reform Jews. Its forms are frankly experimental; it permits a wide latitude in the use of prayers; it has eliminated all references to the Jews as the Chosen People; and it grants equal ritual status to women in the synagogue. Reconstructionism's special emphasis is the belief that Judaism is not only a religion but a religious civilization and it holds that the teachings of Judaism must be reinterpreted and re-evaluated to make them relevant to present-day spiritual and intellectual needs.

Are There Differences in Religious Customs Among Jews in Different Lands?

A COMMON provincialism leads us to assume that the religious customs of our own community are universally observed. A traveler to foreign lands is swiftly disabused of this notion.

The basic rituals in Judaism are universal. The Shema is read in Bagdad as it is in Bangor, Maine, and unleavened bread is the Passover fare for a Jew in Casablanca as it is for his coreligionists in Kansas City. But the customs surrounding each of these religious rites are overhung with so much local coloration that they seem almost alien to the Jewish visitor from another country. A Moroccan Jew would not dream of eating manufactured *matzoth* coming from a factory in Jersey City even though by all ritual standards it is proper for the most pious. His unleavened bread is homemade and circular, not square; and as indigestible as World War I "hard-tack."

Chinese Jews in Cochin are dressed in red silks for the first seven days after marriage—and then in green. In Ceylon an open *Torah* scroll is placed before the bride. In France, I participated in a wedding in which the canopy was made of a *tallith* (this use of the prayer shawl is quite common in Europe).

Even more strange was the custom of making the groom the center of attention rather than the bride!

The Jews of Ethiopia celebrate Passover Eve by slaughtering a paschal lamb and feasting on it. Hayyim Schauss describes the Jews of the Caucasus who "observe Pesach night sitting on the ground dressed in their festive best, with a spear and sometimes a pistol by their sides." Like the Jews of Morocco, they are fond of what we call role-playing—a realistic enactment of the Exodus story by improvised dramatic sketches.

Egyptian Jews have two separate Purim celebrations in the spring: one to mark the Persian story, and the other to commemorate a similar deliverance four hundred years ago.

This tendency on the part of all religious groups to take on local color is disturbing to those who do not understand it. A European Jew visiting a modern American synagogue often sees little difference between the Jewish house of worship and the Christian. He is misled by the superficial aspects of decorum, architectural design and use of a "foreign tongue" to express Sabbath greetings.

The most dramatic evidence of the infinite shades of Jewish expression can be found within the confines of one city—Jerusalem. On a single Saturday morning in a tour of synagogues, one can witness a half-dozen forms of Sabbath worship, including the Yemenite, the Bukharin, the Eastern European, and Hasidic rituals—each with a distinctive character of its own.

The process of cultural assimilation has cast the forms of Jewish ritual expression in a variety of moulds. But these externals do not alter in the slightest the ethical and spiritual unity of the Jewish faith.

Who Were the Pharisees?

THE Pharisees were a political-religious party in ancient Israel at the time when Jesus was born. They represented the middle and lower classes, and therefore were usually found in the ranks of the liberals who believed in worship of God through love, in the simple life and in the equality of all men. The famous rabbi, Hillel, who was among the first to teach that all religion could be summed up in the phrase, "Love thy neighbor," was a Pharisee. When Jesus said, "Judge not lest ye be judged," he was speaking in the ethical tradition of the Pharisees.

The party opposed to the Pharisees were the Sadducees, who reflected the thinking of the upper classes. They were conservative to the point of reaction; they supported absolute monarchy; and were anxious to make peace with Roman tyranny.

In ritual matters, the Pharisees were the most liberal interpreters of religion. The Sadducees insisted on strict observance of the letter of the law, while the Pharisees were willing to reinterpret the law to meet the needs of the time.

Curiously, in the English language, the word Pharisee came to mean just the exact opposite of its original connotation. This switch stems from a misunderstanding of the New Testament. Jesus denounced some of the Pharisees for their hypocrisy in the same manner in which a "Liberal" or a "Democrat" might be reproached for not living up to his name, not out of disapproval of what the Pharisees traditionally stood for.

Actually the preachings of the Pharisees were adopted by Christianity and form an important link between the two religions.

Who Were the Hasidim?

WE USUALLY speak of the Hasidim as a sect within Judaism that began two hundred years ago and flourished in Eastern Europe, particularly in the rural areas. But they were not a sect in the sense of a denomination; they did not secede from the main body of traditional Judaism.

The Hasidim were simply a group of Jews who emphasized a different aspect of the tradition. In a sense, it was a movement of people living in small villages who were not happy with the stress on the intellect rather than the heart. For over a thousand years, Jewish teaching had idealized learning. The scholar was the man closest to God and the greatest sin in the world was ignorance. The Hasidim, in revolt against what they regarded as too much intellectualism, glorified the commonplace.

The founder of the group, Israel Baal Shem Tov, (the last three words are an appellation meaning Good Master of the Name) preached that the ideal worship of God was in simplicity. He could be worshiped in the woods, under a tree, while walking along a country lane.

God demands no temples, declared the Hasidim, but the temple of a sincere heart. Man's prayers need not be clothed in words—but in a devout spirit. One story of the Hasidim tells of an unlettered youngster who sat in the synagogue, softly repeating the alphabet: "Aleph, Beth, Gimel . . ." One of the worshipers asked him the meaning of the strange rite. "You see, I can't read the prayer book," he replied, "so I'm sending up the letters to Heaven. I'm sure that God can put them together in the prayer."

The Hasidim also thought of worship as a thing of joy. Religion must not be too solemn. The equation of pious devotion and a long face was a misunderstanding of true religion. God wants to be worshiped out of happiness—out of a love for His world. Better than the spoken word was the song of prayer. And song accompanied by dance was even more expressive. "All my bones shall declare Thee God," the Bible said. Not only the lips, but the whole body should speak in praise of Him!

It was quite customary among the early Hasidim, on a Sabbath, to sing lusty hymns and dance at the same time. And the influence of Hasidim is still felt in the folk songs which Jews have created in the last century.

The ethical impulse was also a vital part of the Hasidic movement. Communion with God was not a matter of prayer alone, but of acts of love and kindness. "Before prayer, give to charity," is a favorite proverb of the sect. The imaginative Hasidim revived an old mystic tradition that somewhere on earth, at all times, there were thirty-six saints, righteous men who went about their daily business in the disguise of ordinary human beings. They were called *Lamed vov'nicks* (*lamed vov* means thirty-six). The coachman traveling the road to Warsaw; the village blacksmith; the kindergarten teacher—any of them might be one of the thirty-six. Scores of stories were woven about this tradition, all pointing to the moral that one must treat all strangers kindly—for among them might be one of the world's immortals come to test one's religious faith!

The founder of Hasidism was asked by a coachman: "What shall I do about my work? Being a coachman prevents me from attending worship as often as I ought to." "Do you give poor travelers free rides?" the rabbi queried. "Often," said the coachman. "Then keep up your work. You are already serving God."

The leaders of the Hasidic movement, who were regarded with reverent awe by their disciples, were fond of telling parables and stories. Their followers would sit about the table hour after hour while they regaled them with words of *Torah*, weaving into the lessons from the Bible and the *Talmud* vivid anecdotes that illustrated their teachings.

Thousands of such parables and stories have been recorded, and we have a vast treasury of Hasidic tales.

Many of the Hasidic rabbis were noted for their optimistic faith in their fellow men, which could not be weakened in the face of overwhelming evidence of man's perverseness. "Rabbi," one of the disciples complained, "some of the congregants are gossiping in the midst of prayer!" "How wonderful are Thy people, O Lord," the rabbi retorted. "Even in the midst of gossip, they devote a few moments to prayer!"

"Can you tell me, Rabbi, why the wicked are always looking for companions while the righteous do not?" "The answer is simple: a wicked man walks in darkness, and he is anxious for company. A good man walks in the light—and he doesn't mind walking alone."

Unfortunately, the Hasidic movement did not sustain the lofty spiritual level of its founders. In later years they became narrow and Puritanical. But the traditional Hasidic influence served as a leaven, enriching the spirit of Jewish life in the nineteenth and twentieth centuries. The sayings, aphorisms and anecdotes were especially remembered, and became part of the vocabulary of Judaism:

"A city where thieves abound is one which possesses judges who are bribed and police who are corrupt." (Shades of the twentieth century!)

"One who thinks he can live without others is mistaken. One who thinks others cannot live without him is even more mistaken."

"While pursuing happiness we are in flight from contentment."

"Man should be the master of his will and the slave of his conscience."

A tradition that was so warm and down-to-earth inevitably embraced the humorous aspects of life:

"A king visited a prison and talked to the prisoners. Each asserted his innocence, except one who admitted he was a thief. "Throw this scoundrel out," the king ordered, "He will corrupt the innocents."

What Is Cabala?

CABALA (sometimes spelled Kabala) is the mystic tradition in Judaism. The word has made its way into English and other European languages: we use the term, "cabalistic" to mean "mystical" or "mysterious," because there was a time when the Christians of Europe were tremendously interested in this aspect of Judaism.

In the medieval world, many people, Jew and Christian

alike, sought answers to the riddles of the universe in what they regarded as direct and magical communion with God. In the thirteenth century, a Jewish scholar produced a book, supposedly handed down from ancient days, which made use of numbers and letters to explain the teachings of the Bible. It was read avidly by many Jews. Each word and letter of the Sacred Scriptures was carefully weighed, and endowed with special meaning. This was possible because the Hebrew letters of the alphabet have numerical equivalents: the letter "Beth," for example, equals two; the name "Dan" equals fifty-four. Out of these bizarre calculations, the cabalists "figured out" the time of Messiah's approach. Indeed several so-called "Messiahs" appeared, using the authority of Cabala to establish their legitimacy.

There was a great fascination in the tales of the mystics, not unlike the fascination of many contemporaries with the supernatural. Some of the stories of the Cabala had all the elements of suspense, drama, and sometimes the gruesome quality of an Edgar Allan Poe novel. The tale of Aaron the mystic of Bagdad, a ninth century scholar, which appears in an English version in Professor Jacob R. Marcus's *Jew in the Medieval World*, is as intriguing as any modern mystery story. A young man enters a synagogue and ascends to lead in the prayers. His chant is pleasant, but Aaron the mystic is struck by the fact that every time the cantor came to the name of God, he skipped over it. Because of his wide knowledge of Cabala, he challenges the young man: "I know that you are dead . . . and I forbid you to lead our worship. Our Psalms say that the dead may not praise the Lord!"

The youthful cantor breaks down and confesses that he actually is dead, and then recites a long and tangled story to explain his predicament. His death had been predetermined some years ago, but because of the compassion of a rabbi he was kept alive by a mystic device—an incision had been made in his right arm, and the four-lettered name of God had been inserted. Aaron has shrouds brought to the synagogue, and solemnly removes the protective scroll from the young man's arm. Instantly the "dead" man disintegrates before the very eyes of the worshipers and turns to dust.

Oddly enough, this world of Jewish mysticism was the only phase of ghetto learning in which the Christians were interested. Catherine the Great of Russia and other monarchs wanted to learn Hebrew, not as the tongue of the Bible, but as the language of the *Zohar*, the standard book of Cabala.

Despite the emphasis of the mystics on pure speculation, they retained a good measure of the Jewish emphasis on good deeds, on the *practice* of religion. The language of the *Zohar* is often down to earth. Its definition of the intellectual without intelligence is priceless: "He is a donkey laden with books."

The *Zohar* abounds with such sayings as: "The ideal man has the strength of a male and the compassion of a female"; "There is no smoke without fire"; "If a dog is hit with a stone, he bites another dog"; and "In the day of death, a man feels that he has lived but a single day."

Cabala has practically disappeared as an influence in modern Judaism, to whom mysticism has little appeal. But there are faint echoes of its moral teachings in our prayers and traditions.

What Is a Rabbi and What Does He Do?

LITERALLY, a rabbi is a teacher—one who transmits the heritage of his faith to young and old alike. His authority is based not on his position but upon his learning. The rabbi can lay claim to no special privileges, human or divine. He is not in any sense an intermediary between man and God. In Orthodox practice, he rarely leads in the services: it is the cantor who conducts worship, and any well-informed layman may rise to the pulpit to lead in prayer.

A rabbi is identified with the congregation, not with the synagogue. In the community where I was reared, one rabbi served several congregations. He did not preach at regular intervals. He was only required to give two sermons a year: on the Sabbath before Passover and the Sabbath before Yom Kippur. The rabbi's role as a Sabbath preacher is a modern innovation, borrowed from the Protestants.

There is no religious hierarchy in the Jewish faith. The influence of the individual rabbi is determined solely by his ability to gain and keep the respect of laymen and colleagues as an interpreter of Jewish law and tradition.

The title, rabbi, was first used nineteen hundred years ago. Before that time, scholars of the stature of Hillel bore no title. Even today, in referring to the wise man of antiquity, it is customary to omit the honorary prefix. It would be an anachronism to speak of "Rabbi Hillel"; yet his immediate successors are called rabbis.

The modern American rabbi is a graduate of a recognized *yeshivah* or seminary, and completes a course of religious studies on a postgraduate level. Reform and Conservative seminaries require a Bachelor's degree before acceptance as a freshman student. Four or five years of graduate studies are the minimum prerequisite for ordination. In addition to his religious training, the rabbinical student must equip himself in the social sciences, particularly in psychology, sociology, general history and English; he must pass a psychiatric test, and he must convince the examining board of his earnest desire to become a teacher and interpreter of the Jewish tradition.

The modern Orthodox seminary is less exacting in its demands for secular education; studies are concentrated on the fields of talmudic learning and Jewish law. The oldest and largest school, the Rabbi Isaac Elchanan Seminary in New York City, commonly referred to as simply "the Yeshivah," also requires a college degree before ordination, and provides training in the social sciences.

Marriage is not only permitted to the rabbi; according to Jewish law it is required. The rabbi's wife, affectionately called the *rebbetzin*, assumes a place in synagogue life comparable to that of the wife who presides over the home of the Protestant parish. She is expected to take an active part in congregational activities; she may, on occasion, teach in the religious school, and frequently she serves as a counselor, not only for the rabbi's flock, but for the rabbi himself.

The modern rabbi's duties parallel those of his Protestant colleagues. He is responsible for religious education, for synagogue worship, for preaching, for ceremonials surrounding birth, confirmation, marriage and death in the lives of his congregants, and for pastoral guidance. And his success is measured primarily in terms of the trust, friendship and affection he enjoys among his followers.

What Is a Cantor?

To UNDERSTAND the duties of a cantor one must have a clear picture of the general procedure in Jewish worship.

Prayers are not read by the congregants; they are chanted. The cantor intones the first few words of a prayer, which serves as a cue for the congregation to continue it individually. At the end of the congregational chant, the cantor again intones the last verse or two aloud. If the prayer ends in a blessing, the congregation responds with "Blessed be He and blessed His name, Amen." The cantor then continues with the first few words of the next prayer.

It is perfectly proper for any member of the congregation to serve as cantor, if he is familiar with the ritual. But for a number of centuries the larger synagogues have retained a special person for this task. In recent centuries, as the liturgy became more elaborate, greater emphasis was placed on musical quality in the chanting of prayers, and the cantor assumed a more important place in worship. Since instrumental music was forbidden by tradition (see p. 137), the beauty of the services could only be enhanced by a cantor with a well-trained voice. Although the synagogue melodies were not written music, there was an established mode or pattern for each occasion, so distinctive that a worshiper entering the synagogue could tell by the melody alone whether it was a Sabbath Passover, Rosh Hashanah or ordinary weekday service. The cantor was therefore required to be familiar with the traditional motifs, and fewer laymen were equipped to do justice to the ritual.

In times past, the cantor's duties often covered a variety of other functions: he read the *Torah*, supervised the physical care of the synagogue, taught the children elementary Hebrew, and on occasion preached a sermon as well. An old law recommended that if a congregation could not afford both a cantor and a rabbi, the cantor was to be preferred.

In our own day, most Orthodox and Conservative synagogues engage a full-time cantor, whose responsibilities include choral direction, religious education, particularly in preparation for the Bar Mitzvah ceremony, and occasionally some of the administrative functions of a congregation.

The cantor's role in Reform worship is more limited, and is usually a part-time position.

During the past three years, both the Reform and Conservative movements in the United States have established schools which train students to fulfill the duties of cantor, musical director and educator.

What Is the Difference Between a Synagogue and a Temple?

THE words synagogue and temple are largely interchangeable. Neither are Hebrew terms: synagogue comes from the Greek for "bringing together" and temple from the Latin "templum." A generation ago, "temple" was used to denote a modern religious institution, and "synagogue" referred to an Orthodox house of worship. Today these distinctions hardly apply. In some communities the temple is Conservative while the Reform congregation is called a synagogue.

As the Greek derivation suggests, a synagogue is more than a place of prayer. It is a gathering place—the focal point of all Jewish community life. In addition to being a sanctuary for worship, it serves as the home of religious education, youth activities and social affairs. For many centuries, the synagogue also contained a hostel for wayfarers.

The modern Jewish house of worship was originally called a temple because it was established almost exclusively as a house of prayer. But as its complexion altered, the word expanded in meaning. A Jewish temple today like the synagogue is synonymous with the entire gamut of religious, cultural and social activities of a congregation.

What Are the Most Important Symbols in the Synagogue?

SEVERAL of the symbols found in the synagogue are as old as the Jewish religion.

The most conspicuous symbol, placed over the Ark, is the tablet containing the first two words of each of the Ten Commandments. The Moral Law, cornerstone of Judaism, thus occupies a central place in the synagogue.

The seven-branched candelabrum, the *menorah*, harks back to the days of the Sanctuary in the wilderness, described in the

Book of Exodus. When the Temple of Solomon was erected, ten tall imposing golden candelabra stood in the central hall of worship in commemoration of the Sanctuary *menorah*.

The Eternal Light, an oil lamp which hangs before the Ark of the *Torah*, also antedates the Temple of Solomon. The flame that never dies represents the continuity of Jewish tradition, as well as God's eternal presence.

With few exceptions, the Orthodox synagogue is constructed so that its worshipers always face eastward—toward Jerusalem—during prayer. In most Orthodox synagogues, too, the pulpit stand is in the center of the Sanctuary, so that the person leading the worship is a participant, joining his fellow worshipers rather than standing apart from them. Reform and Conservative synagogues, and a few Orthodox as well, have their pulpit stands in front of the Ark.

Most modern synagogues also use other symbols, largely for decorative purposes. Frescoes and murals usually depict festival and holy day symbols such as the *shofar*, the *megillah*, and the palm branch, or scenes from the Bible. The lions of Judah, symbol of the ancient House of David, are seen in some Orthodox synagogues.

Is Instrumental Music Prohibited in the Synagogue?

IN THE ancient Temple at Jerusalem, the sound of the harp the clanging cymbals and the horns mingled with stringed instruments and the voices of the Levites' chorus in the praise of God.

With the destruction of the Temple, however, the use of instrumental music in worship fell out of favor. One reason for this was the development of a synagogue ritual of prayers and blessings. The worshiper could hardly do justice to the prayers and play an instrument at the same time. A second reason for the prohibition against music in the synagogue was to mourn the destruction of the Temple and the Golden Age of Israel which it represented. For if music was a part of the ritual in the joyous days, the lack of music served as a reminder to Jews of their lost heritage. Thus, for over a thousand years, no musical instrument was heard in accompaniment to Jewish worship.

Very gradually, during the middle ages, the prohibition was made less stringent. In the thirteenth century, the Bagdad synagogue permitted organ music during the Middle Days of Passover and Tabernacles. But it took another five hundred years before the Reform synagogues finally lifted the ban.

By the nineteenth century, some Orthodox congregations in Germany, Italy and France joined with the Reform group in reintroducing music at worship. But American synagogues, all except the Reform, were hesitant about the "new" practice. Many worshipers came from Eastern Europe, where the organ and other means of music were considered inappropriate for the solemn atmosphere of the synagogue. Besides that, choral music had been developed to such an elaborate degree that instrumental accompaniment was hardly missed.

In the past few years some Conservative American congregations have begun to use the organ during worship. But only the Reform groups have allowed stringed and brass instruments as well.

Why Are Most Synagogue Services Conducted in Hebrew?

ACCORDING to Jewish law, one may pray in any language. Indeed, many Reform and Conservative groups use a good deal of English in their prayers. But there is a tremendous emotional satisfaction in repeating a prayer in the same language used by our forefathers. The Hebrew language links the Jews of all countries to one another and to their common heritage. To translate the Shema into another language would be to detach it a little from its three-thousand-year history.

Retaining Hebrew as the language of prayer also preserves the universal character of the Jewish faith. Recently, I attended services in the Grand Synagogue of Rome. As soon as I entered the Temple, I felt myself a part of the congregation. I don't think this would have been possible if the services had been conducted in Italian. I would have felt alien to the worship, even though I sat in a Jewish house of God. But the familiar sounds of the Hebrew prayers gave me a feeling of kinship with my fellow Jews in that synagogue, thousands of miles from my home.

In the third place, the use of Hebrew in worship has provided Jews with a stimulus to study the language, to learn the tongue of the Bible. In the most expert translation, something precious evaporates—for a language is the mirror of a people's soul. Hebrew scholarship would have ceased to exist had there not been this life-preserving impulse to keep alive the original prayers of the Synagogue.

Even those who do not understand the exact meaning of the Hebrew words usually develop a "feeling" for the prayers. The solemnity of the Kol Nidre, for example—the soulful liturgy which the Cantor chants to usher in the Day of Atonement is *understood* by most Jews, regardless of their familiarity with the actual language (in this case, mostly Aramaic). A number of years ago, some Liberal synagogues eliminated the Kol Nidre from the Yom Kippur services. But in recent years they have decided to restore it because of its rich historical associations. Apparently they discovered that the individual phrases were not as important as the prayer as a whole.

As a matter of fact, many people find it easier to pray in a language they do not use in their everyday lives. It is the mood rather than the intellectual content which human beings seek in worship.

What Is a Mezuzah?

A MEZUZAH is literally a doorpost, but it has come to signify the small wooden, metal or glass case, about three inches in length, which is placed on the doorpost of a Jewish home. "Thou shalt find the words of the Law for a sign . . . upon thy door," commands the Bible.

The *mezuzah* is usually set at an angle, about five feet from the floor, to the right of the entrance. In Orthodox and Conservative homes we find them on every door in the house.

Inside the case is a tiny parchment on which are inscribed fifteen verses from the book of Deuteronomy. The first sentence is the watchword of Israel, "Hear O Israel, the Lord our God, is One." The inscription continues with the command to "love God and to serve Him with all thy heart, with all thy soul," and ends with a reminder that God's laws must be instilled in our children at home and away from home.

For those who live in the house, the *mezuzah* is a constant reminder of God's presence. They see it as they enter, assuring them that He is there, and they see it as they leave, reminding them that His watchful care is everywhere. To the passer-by, the *mezuzah* is a token that the home is Jewish—and one that is marked by the love of God.

Israel Abrahams, in his Commentary on the Prayer Book, suggests that the original practice may have been borrowed from the ancient Egyptians, who wrote "lucky sentences" over the entrance of their homes. But, as with many other traditions which can be traced back to primitive roots, Judaism has endowed this custom with a great deal of meaning, and has transmuted a bit of superstition into a profound ethical symbol.

What Significance Has the Shield of David?

THE Shield of David, or *Mogen David*, is a six-pointed star made up of two triangles pointing in opposite directions. The star has no ancient Jewish origin or religious meaning. It became a popular symbol in Jewish life about three hundred years ago in Central Europe.

A medieval mystic declared that the six-pointed star was identical to the royal shield of the House of David, while the five-pointed star resembled the "Seal of Solomon." Although the idea was just a figment of cabalistic imagination, it was gradually accepted as true and the Shield of David took on a very special significance for the Jewish community.

Whatever its origin, the Shield of David has become a distinctively Jewish symbol. The Nazis ordered it worn by Jews as a "badge of shame." John Hersey's novel of the Warsaw Ghetto, "The Wall," describes a moving scene in which the valiant women of the Ghetto vied with one another in sewing these badges in the most expensive materials they could find, and competed in creating the most beautiful design. But though it often stirs deep emotions of loyalty and pride, the six-pointed star cannot be considered in any sense a sacred symbol.

In recent times, the star is frequently found as a decoration in synagogue architecture. And the growth of Zionism in the last seventy-five years gave it national significance. The flag of modern Israel is a white banner, with two horizontal blue bars, and between them a blue Shield of David.

Why Are Jews Called 'The People of the Book'?

IT WAS Mohammed, founder of Islam, who first called the Jews the People of the Book—and The Book he referred to was the Bible. Mohammed was tremendously impressed with the Old Testament and felt certain that the people who produced the Holy Scriptures must have qualities of greatness.

In more modern times the phrase "people of the book" has also been used to describe the traditional love of learning in Jewish life. For throughout Jewish history, study was the most respected task and scholarship the greatest mark of achievement. Only a learned man could know the Law as God gave it to Moses on Mount Sinai. Ignorance was therefore a sacrilege—an offense against the very basis of the Jewish religion.

Thus, in days when almost all of Eastern Europe was a sea of illiteracy, there was rarely a Jew who could not read well enough to follow the prayers in the synagogue. The poorest family somehow managed to send their five- or six-year-old boys to school to learn the rudiments of Hebrew and the *Torah*. And when there was no family, the entire community undertook the elementary education of the orphan child, as it undertook, also, the higher learning and support of every youngster promising in his studies.

The Bible was the textbook of the common people. Professor Abraham Heschel, describing Old World Jewry, pictures its synagogues as "full of all classes busily engaged in studies, townsfolk as well as young men from afar . . . where at dusk, between twilight and evening prayers, artisans and other simple folk gather around the tables to listen to a discourse on the great books of the *Torah*, to interpretations of Scriptures . . . and the like."

This attachment to the Bible was carried over in Judaism to a broad respect for the printed word. In the Orthodox synagogue or religious school, even today, a youngster who has accidentally dropped a book will lift it from the floor to his lips and kiss it as atonement for the desecration. For books are considered the fountain of learning; they are to be embraced as something precious. A home unadorned with bookshelves is lifeless and lacking in a soul.

Love of learning, therefore, originally of the wisdom of The Book, the Bible, and later, of all knowledge wherever it might be found, has earned for the Jews the honored title, People of the Book.

VI

FEASTS AND FASTS

> *Whenever the Israelites on earth rejoice in the festivals, give praise to the Lord, adorn the table with viands and don fine garments, the angels above inquire: "Why do Israelites pamper themselves so much?" God replies: "They have a distinguished guest with them today."*
>
> THE *Zohar*

Feasts and Fasts

RABBI JOSHUA, in the second century, declared, "Half of the festivals shall be spent on feasting, and half on prayer."

That sentiment has prevailed in Jewish tradition down through the ages. The festive days all include a judicious mixture of lightheartedness and solemnity, deftly interwoven. Passover is a time for children's games—but it is also the occasion for worship: "Bestow upon us the blessing of Thy holy festivals for life and peace . . ." Simchath Torah, despite its gay spirit, is a time for supplication: "O Lord our God, be with us as Thou wast with our fathers; leave us not, forsake us not."

The sacred days of the Jewish year are largely a matter of atmosphere—a feeling created and even contrived to establish a mood that gave each festive or solemn day its unique character.

Actually, each holiday represented a *season* rather than an individual *day* or cluster of days. Passover begins, in a sense, the day after Purim—a month before the actual Feast. This is the season of spring cleaning—but it is more than the annual farewell to winter. The mother, busy with her additional chores, is very conscious that "before we know it, Passover will be here." There is a sense of expectancy that is conveyed to the whole family. This feeling grows during the entire month. By the Eve of Passover, both home and family are spiritually prepared for the great days.

At the close of the festival, there is reminiscence: comments on how smoothly the five-year-old "baby" of the family recited the Four Questions at the *Seder* table, the unusual flavor of the food, the special guests.

This lengthy savoring of each event lends to every occasion a threefold enrichment. First, there is the zest of anticipation; then the actual experience, and finally the joys of reminiscence. It would be very difficult to select among these that phase of the celebration which holds most meaning, which contributes most to the fullness of life.

It must also be kept in mind that the Jewish holidays are more than mere celebrations or even commemorations. They serve as object lessons in Judaism's most important ideals: thanksgiving, freedom, learning and wisdom, sacrifice, repentance. The holy days dramatize these values, and give them substance, particularly for the young.

Abstract values are always difficult to teach. A love of learning is transmitted to a child more clearly through the pageantry of the *Torah* processional on the feast of Simchath Torah, than it could possibly be in a classroom lesson. For in this way he learns, even at an early age, that the teachings of the Bible are sacred to his family and his group and they are precious objects of affection.

The festivals also serve the very useful function of strengthening family and group bonds. For be it fast or feast, a Jewish holy day is the season of homecoming. And if home with the family is impossible, home with the group—with others of the same faith—is next best. A Jewish soldier stationed in Arizona exhausts every possible means of joining his family at the *Seder* table, be it in Boston or Seattle. And if he can't, he looks for a

Seder table nearby. Overseas, during World War II, I saw soldiers flock to the synagogues on even a minor festival like *Purim*. In the synagogue of Algiers, the worshipers vied with one another for the privilege of inviting Jewish G.I.'s for the Purim feast. And the soldiers accepted eagerly and gratefully. The food was rather exotic, and the customs different than those they knew in the United States—but it was a touch of home, nevertheless, and on Purim (or Passover or Rosh Hashanah) one felt an overpowering need to be home.

During the second century, a Gentile asked Rabbi Akiba: "In the prophecies of Isaiah, the Lord says: 'I despise your feasts.' Why then, do you celebrate them?" The rabbi replied: "You will notice that God said, '*your* feasts' and not '*My* feasts.' If the festive days are used for the sake of man alone, they are worthless. But if they are attached to things divine, they have meaning and value."

Why Do Jewish Holidays Fall on Different Days Each Year?

JEWISH holidays are reckoned on the Jewish calendar, which differs from the Georgian calendar used by most of the western world.

The Jewish calendar is based on a lunar year, running 354 or 355 days, rather than the solar year of the Gregorian calendar which runs 365 or 366 days. For that reason, Jewish holidays which always fall on the same date of the Jewish calendar come out on different dates of the Gregorian calendar every year. Seven times in nineteen years, an entire additional month is added to the Jewish calendar for a leap year.

The names of the Jewish months were borrowed, as in the modern calendar, from pagan sources and are actually Babylonian in origin. Only remnants of old Hebrew names are found in the Bible.

Rosh Hashanah (see p. 154) ushers in the Jewish New Year. In September, 1952, Rosh Hashanah marked the beginning of the year 5713 of our calendar. According to tradition, the year 1 was the year of Creation, though modern Jews interpret this as the dawn of civilization rather than of the world.

It is interesting to note that of the three major faiths Judaism alone reckons its calendar not from an event in its own history, but from what it considers the birth date of all mankind.

Why Do Jews Fast on Certain Days?

FASTING has three distinct purposes in the Jewish faith, self-denial, mourning and petition.

In addition to Yom Kippur (see p. 156) several minor fasts are observed by the Orthodox, the most important of which is the Day of Lamentation, Tisha B'ab, in August, which commemorates the destruction of both of the Temples of Jerusalem. The period of fasting is usually twenty-four hours, from sunset of one day to sunset of the next.

On the Day of Atonement fasting is the symbol of man's ability to conquer his physical appetites—a demonstration to God that the individual is able to deny the natural cravings for food and drink and will also try to control all of his selfish desires.

As a sign of mourning, fasting expresses either collective sorrow or individual grief. The fast of Lamentation recalls to the Jew the destruction of his ancient homeland. The Orthodox Jew also refrains from food and drink on the anniversary of the death of a parent. When I visited Palestine in 1936 during the Arab riots, the Jerusalem rabbinate proclaimed a day of public fasting to express sympathy for the fallen victims.

Fasting as a form of prayer was customary when disaster struck the Jewish community. In the face of a plague or threatened destruction, the leaders called upon the people to join them in fasting. The Book of Esther tells that when Haman threatened to destroy the Jews of Persia, Queen Esther undertook to save her people and sent word to them, "Fast ye for me." Among very observant Jews the day before the Feast of Purim is still marked by fasting.

Although asceticism is generally frowned upon in Jewish tradition, it has been the custom among very pious Jews to fast on many occasions throughout the year, particularly on Mondays or Thursdays, when special penitential prayers are recited according to tradition.

What Does the Sabbath Mean to Jews?

THE Sabbath is more than an institution in Judaism. It is *the* institution of the Jewish religion.

A historian could write two histories of the Jews, one bearing little resemblance to the other. The external history, that is, how they have fared socially and politically through the years, is a rather dismal chronicle of persecution, expulsion and dispersion. But the spiritual history of the Jews—the strength they were able to fashion out of their environment—is another story. For somehow they managed to create a life which gave them not only spiritual satisfaction and the determination to continue as a group, but a sense of well-being in the midst of a troubled world.

Without a doubt, the Sabbath was at the very heart of this inner world of peace and serenity. There is the saying: "More than Israel kept the Sabbath, the Sabbath kept Israel." For Jewish spiritual history was virtually a series of weekdays spent in preparation for the Sabbath.

This is no mere figure of speech. The traditional life of the Jew was bound up in his Sabbath. The other six days were a means to an end—a man worked only to enable him to reap the joys of the Sabbath.

In the hustle and bustle of modern living, many non-Jews—and even non-observant Jews—see the Sabbath as a day hemmed in by all kinds of restrictions—when driving a car is taboo, buying a newspaper is forbidden and writing a letter is a violation of the law. But the observant do not think of the Sabbath as a time when they are prevented from performing all sorts of minor labors, but rather as a twenty-four hour period when they can enjoy a world of complete serenity, beauty and peace.

Sabbath is a time for spiritual refreshment, and for a break in the monotonous routine of daily labor. It is a reminder that the need for making a living must not blind us to the need for living.

Sabbath is also a family day made for memories—when children who have grown up and married rejoin their family circle; when grandparents, parents and youngsters share in the feeling of oneness as the children bow their heads and the father repeats a blessing: "May the Lord bless thee and keep thee on this Sabbath day." It is a day with all kinds of bright embellishments: special foods; twisted loaves of bread; sweet wine for the Sabbath blessing; fresh white tablecloth; flickering white candles; the best china and silverware; flowers in a polished vase; and young and old alike decked out in their best finery.

A glance at the history of the Sabbath reveals that its character grew with the centuries. Some sects among the medieval Jews pressed for the observance of a somber Sabbath. A group known as the Karaites (of whom there are but a remnant in the Mediterranean region) insisted that God wanted the Sabbath to be lifeless and lightless, since the Bible said, "Thou shalt not kindle a flame on the Sabbath day." But the wiser tradition prevailed, and the day gradually developed into a Sabbath of joy. Professor Abraham Heschel suggests, quoting an old tradition, that "Thou shalt not kindle a flame" refers to the flame of anger. The Sabbath called for even tempers and pleasant dispositions, for spiritual joy, based on such enduring values as learning, family love and preoccupation with things of the soul.

The Sabbath is, of course, a day of synagogue worship. The Orthodox usher in the Sabbath before sundown on Friday, and attend services before dinner. Conservative and Reform Jews attend a late evening service, and participate in an *oneg shabbat*, an hour of sociability after worship.

All three groups have Saturday morning worship, during which a portion of the *Torah* is read. Among the Orthodox and Conservative Jews, a Sabbath afternoon service is also held, and a portion of the *Torah* for the following week is recited.

Although the rituals differ somewhat among the three wings of American Judaism, their prayers are variations of a single theme. The Orthodox and Conservative pray: "Our God and God of our fathers, may our rest be acceptable unto Thee; hallow us by Thy commandments, satisfy us with Thy goodness and gladden us with Thy salvation; O purify our hearts to serve Thee in truth. . . ."

And there are few prayers more eloquent or more descriptive of the Sabbath than the Reform prayer, chanted during the Kiddush (sanctification over wine): "Let us praise God with this symbol of joy, and thank Him for the blessings of the past week, for life and strength, for home and love and friendship, for the discipline of our trials and temptations, for the happiness that has come to us out of our labors. Thou hast ennobled us, O God, with the blessings of work, and in love hast sanctified us by Sabbath rest and worship. . . ."

Rosh Hashanah

ROSH HASHANAH is Hebrew for New Year. It marks one of the two most sacred holy days in the Jewish faith and ushers in the Ten Days of Penitence when "mankind passes in judgment before the heavenly throne." During this period, tradition holds, God looks into the hearts of men and examines not only their deeds but their motives as well. It is also the period when Jews sit in judgment over themselves, comparing their conduct during the past year with the hopes and resolutions they had cherished.

Like the Christian Easter, which also follows the Jewish

calendar (see p. 149), Rosh Hashanah falls on a different date each year. Reform groups and the Jews of modern Israel celebrate Rosh Hashanah for one day; Orthodox and Conservative Jews continue to observe two equally holy days, as has been the custom since the first century.

Along with almost every other Jewish holy day, the Rosh Hashanah observances include a mixture of solemnity and festivity. The New Year is a time for a gathering of the clan, when young and old alike return to the family hearth. The pageantry of our holy day rituals creates emotional bonds to Judaism even among children too young to fully understand and appreciate the ethics of our faith. In later years the intellect re-enforces these bonds of the mind and heart.

The most important symbol of the Rosh Hashanah observances is the *shofar*, or ram's horn, which is sounded during worship on the New Year and each of the ten days of penitence. In ancient times, the *shofar* was an instrument of communication. In the hills of Judaea it was possible to reach the entire country in a matter of moments with *shofar* calls from a row of mountain peaks. In the Rosh Hashanah services, the *shofar* is the call to worship. It calls upon the faithful to repent for their misdeeds of the past year; to return to God with contrite and humble spirit and to distinguish between the trivial and the important in life, so that the next twelve months may be richer in service to God and man.

In spite of the solemn nature of the Rosh Hashanah observances, there is a general air of happy expectancy in home and synagogue. We enter the Ten Days of Penitence with faith in God's compassion and forgiveness. A significant Rosh Hashanah blessing gives thanks to God "for having kept us in health, and sustained us to reach this day." And in the prayers that accompany the breaking of bread, the bread is dipped in honey as a symbol of the sweetness which we hope will mark the new year.

Among the variety of meanings which Jews assign to Rosh Hashanah is "the birthday of the world"—the anniversary of Creation. And among the day's prayers is one looking to the day when "all men shall come to serve Thee"—when mankind will be joined in universal brotherhood under the Fatherhood of God.

Yom Kippur

> For the sin which we have committed against Thee
>   under stress or through choice;
> For the sin which we have committed against Thee
>   in stubbornness or in error;
> For the sin which we have committed against Thee
>   in the evil meditations of the heart;
> For the sin which we have committed against Thee
>   by word of mouth;
> For the sin which we have committed against Thee
>   by abuse of power; . . .
> For the sin which we have committed against Thee
>   by exploiting and dealing treacherously
>   with our neighbor . . .
> For all these sins, O God of forgiveness, bear
>   with us, pardon us, forgive us!

THIS is the prayer which runs through the entire service on Yom Kippur. Yom Kippur is the Day of Atonement, the last of the Ten Days of Penitence, and, like Rosh Hashanah, one of the two High Holy Days of Judaism. It is marked by twenty-four hours of prayer and fasting. As the sun begins to set on the Eve of Atonement, the family gathers for a festive meal. Candles are lit, and members of the family ask forgiveness of one another for the wrongs they have committed, child of parent, parent of child, and husband and wife of each other. For we must enter the sacred day with a clean slate.

White, symbol of purity, is the dominant color of Yom Kippur. The altar cloths and *Torah* covers in the synagogue, maroon on the Sabbaths and blue on the festivals, are changed to white. The rabbi and cantor wear white robes, and in some Conservative congregations all the men wear white skull caps.

The Kol Nidre chant, led by the cantor, is the prelude to the Day of Atonement and is recited just before the sun sets. It is a prayer for absolution, asking God to release us from vows undertaken, but not fulfilled. These vows refer only to man's promises to God—not to his fellow-men. All the prayers of Yom Kippur cannot absolve a man from sins against his neighbor: only a forgiving neighbor can do so.

A constant refrain throughout the day is the prayer: "Father we have sinned before Thee," and the worshiper recounts the traditional catalogue of sins, shortcomings and transgressions that cover the wide gamut of human dereliction.

The Yom Kippur confessional is deliberately recited in terms of "we," not "I." There are individual sins, of course, but there is also an acceptance of collective responsibility for the shortcomings of mankind. On Yom Kippur we share each other's burden of guilt.

But solemn as the day may be, there is still an element of joy in Yom Kippur—the joy that comes with the thought of forgiveness. We believe that "God is nigh unto the brokenhearted" and that, in the words of the Yom Kippur ritual, "Thou desirest not the death of the wicked, but that he return from his sin, and live." Therefore the pious Jew trusts implicitly in his mercy and forgiveness.

Judaism stresses that prayer is not the sole avenue of God's grace. Equally important, always, in God's eyes, are deeds of love and compassion.

A story is told of Rabbi Israel Salanter, one of the most distinguished Orthodox rabbis of the nineteenth century. One Yom Kippur eve the rabbi failed to appear for worship to intone the sacred Kol Nidre prayer. His congregation was worried, for it was inconceivable that their saintly rabbi would be late or absent on this holy of holiest days! A search party was organized to scour the countryside. After a long search they found their rabbi, in the barn of a Christian neighbor. On his way to worship, he had come upon one of his neighbor's calves lost and tangled in the brush. Tenderly he freed it, and led the calf back to his stall. That night of Yom Kippur the rabbi's prayer was an act of mercy.

The Feast of Succoth

Succoth is the Festival of Tabernacles, which begins five days after the Day of Atonement and continues for eight days (seven for Reform Jews). It is a harvest festival of thanksgiving—a reminder of the celebration in ancient Palestine when the crops had been gathered and the rainy season was approaching.

The feast is a gay and happy event, full of rich and colorful symbols, and especially appealing to children, for whom it is obviously intended. A booth or hut (*succah*) is erected near the home. This is usually an improvised structure of wooden boards, with a roof of leaves and branches. The roof must not be solid, for those in the *succah* must be able to see the sky at all times. The building of a booth is prescribed in the Bible, as an eternal reminder of the temporary dwellings used by the Israelites in their forty years of wandering through the wilderness. The interior of the *succah* is gaily decorated with fruits of the autumn season and furnished with a table and chairs. During the week of Succoth the family meal is served in the *succah*.

Two other symbols mark the festival of Succoth: the citron (a fruit which is cousin to the lemon), and the *lulav*, a palm branch tied around with myrtle and willows. Each plant has its symbolic meaning, but essentially, like the *succah*, they recall man's dependence on the soil and his obligations to Him who causes the earth to yield its bounty.

Although the individual family *succah* has often given way to the community or synagogue *succah*, many Jews still preserve the original custom.

Building the booth always occasions great excitement. In my own family the project is a neighborhood affair: all the children of the block, Jewish, Catholic and Protestant, share in the construction. My children and their friends begin their labors immediately after sunset on the Day of Atonement. Wood is hauled, measured, cut, nailed together. Leaves and branches are taken from trees in the neighborhood; corn stalks are brought in from the nearest farm, and fruits are tied to strings to be hung from the ceiling and on the walls.

Special services are held in the synagogue on the first two

days and the last two days of Succoth (the first and last day in the Reform ritual). The theme of all the prayers is thanksgiving and as the traditional blessings are repeated, the congregants march in a processional circle, bearing the palm branch and the citron (*ethrog*).

Simchath Torah

THE festival of Simchath Torah is celebrated at the close of Succoth, and is dedicated to the glorification of the *Torah*. This is the day when the weekly readings of the Five Books of Moses are completed for the year and the synagogue begins the *Torah* readings afresh.

On Simchath Torah, the worshipers read the last chapters of the Book of Deuteronomy and immediately afterwards the first chapter of Genesis, symbolizing the everlasting continuity of Judaism. The *Torah* is eternal, this ritual declares; therefore it has no real beginning—no real end.

Despite the solemnity of this symbolism, the festival of Simchath Torah has become the gayest day of the year. It is a time for feasting and, among the Hasidim, an occasion for exuberant dancing.

On the eve of Simchath Torah an elaborate service is held. The scrolls are removed from the Ark, and given to the congregation. Each worshiper, young and old, takes his turn in carrying a Scroll in a processional around the pews. The children carry banners, kiss the *Torah* scrolls, and receive candies and other sweets. During morning worship, the ceremony is repeated, in a somewhat more solemn vein.

The honor of being called to the reading of the last verses of the Torah is given to a distinguished member of the congregation, who is referred to as the "Bridegroom of the *Torah*." The congregant who is called to the reading of Genesis is named the "Bridegroom of the Beginning."

Today, some congregations also designate a "Bride of the Scriptures," honoring a woman who is summoned to read the lesson from the Prophets.

The Feast of Hanukkah

HANUKKAH, or the Feast of Lights, is observed in December for a period of eight days, and commemorates Israel's victory in the first recorded battle for religious liberty. As Dr. Theodore Gaster points out, it is the spiritual counterpart of the Purim celebration, for while Purim commemorates the rescue of the Jews from physical destruction at the hands of an oppressor, *Hanukkah* marks the rescue of Judaism, as a faith and a way of life, from obliteration.

The story of Hanukkah is the story of the Maccabees, who in 168 B.C.E. led a small, inspired army of Jews against the overwhelming might of their Syrian rulers in a struggle to the death for the right to worship God in their own traditional way. It is a valiant story which has filled generations of Jews with a justifiable pride in their heritage. Yet Jewish tradition was hesitant about transforming a military triumph into a religious celebration. For although the Bible regarded some wars as just, it did not allow human bloodshed to be associated with worship. King David, one of Judaism's greatest heroes, was not permitted to build the Temple, because his life had been devoted to the pursuits of war.

The ancient rabbis therefore laid greatest emphasis on the spiritual aspects of the Maccabean war. This is why during the Feast of Hanukkah the prophecy of Zechariah is read: "Not by strength, nor by power, but by My spirit, saith the Lord of hosts." And to the Silent Devotion is added the thanksgiving: "For the miracles of liberation which Thou hast wrought . . . Thou didst deliver the strong into the hands of the weak, and the arrogant into the hands of those devoted to Thy Law."

The symbolism of the Feast is completely devoid of military references. Candles are lit for eight successive evenings by either parent (some families permit the children to take their turn) in a Hanukkah *menorah* especially designed for the Feast of Lights. One candle is lit the first evening, two the second, and so on until all eight are kindled. An additional candle, called the *shammos*, is lit at the same time, to be used to kindle the other tapers. In ancient times it was suggested that the order of kindling be inversed: eight candles the first night, seven the second, etc. But the rabbis of the School of Hillel clung to the procedure which has now become fixed, to reflect Israel's faith in a brighter future.

The extra candle was also endowed with special meaning. The flame gives of itself to create an additional flame without losing any of its own brightness. Thus man gives of his love to his fellow men without losing anything of himself.

American Jews have transmuted this minor festival into a major one largely because its traditional customs so closely parallel the Christmas celebration which occurs at the same time. Hanukkah had always been a time for festivity, for games and parties, for special seasonal dishes and for gifts to the children. In imitation of the general atmosphere prevailing in December, Hanukkah is now marked by exchanges of gifts for young and old, and homes are gaily decorated with a variety of Hanukkah symbols.

There are traditional blessings, songs and hymns for the Hanukkah season. "Rock of Ages" (not to be confused with the Christian hymn) is probably the most popular and most widely known hymn.

During these weeks the synagogue religious school takes on a festive air. Pageants, plays and musical operettas, all based on the theme of the Maccabean victory and religious liberty, are carefully rehearsed and presented.

The growing importance of Hanukkah in American Jewish life is an excellent example of the changing traditions in Judaism, altered, not by law, but by life itself. As Rabbi Solomon Schechter pointed out a half-century ago, these changes are not a sign of disintegration of faith, but reflect the vitality of an evergrowing tradition.

The Feast of Purim

PURIM is the carnival festival of Jewish life, a carefree day of rejoicing for the spectacular events recorded in the Book of Esther.

Each year, in February or March, Purim recalls the plot of Haman to destroy the Jews of Persia—and the bravery of Queen Esther and the wisdom of Mordecai, who, together, saved their people from death.

Purim is a time for masquerade parties, a custom borrowed from Christian neighbors who celebrate their Mardi Gras at about the same time. The carnival idea itself is neither Christian nor Jewish, but dates back to some primitive early spring celebration.

The Purim celebration has been a kind of safety valve for Jews suffering under the yoke of persecution. They would gather in the synagogue on the eve of Purim and listen to the dramatic events portrayed in the *megillah* (scroll) of Esther. Whenever Haman's name was mentioned, the children would set up a din with noisemakers to express their condemnation of the villain. After the reading, sweet cakes would be passed around, gifts exchanged and bounties disbursed to the poor.

The *megillah* itself has always been a beautiful and intricately illustrated manuscript. Jewish artists, limited by the ban against the making of images, expressed some of their finest talents in such synagogue objects as the *megillah*.

Many beautifully illuminated scrolls of the Middle Ages have been preserved, as well as the metal cases which contained them. These cases were often made of silver filigree of exquisite design and represent a craftsmanship and artistry of very high order.

With all its gay abandon, Purim is also a day of spiritual comfort, a reminder that tyrants perish and that evil can gain only a temporary victory in man's struggle for freedom.

Among very Orthodox Jews it is customary to fast on the day before the Feast of Purim in remembrance of the fast ordered by Queen Esther when she prayed for her people's safety. The fast is not strictly observed, today, however, except among the Jews of modern Persia.

The Meaning of Passover

PASSOVER, or Pesach as it is called in Hebrew, is the outstanding home festival in Jewish life. It is the Feast of Freedom, commemorating Israel's deliverance from Egyptian bondage.

Passover is celebrated for eight days (seven days by Reform Jews) during the first month of spring.

The rituals of Passover are largely home ceremonials. On the day before the holiday begins, the house is examined from basement to attic for any sign of leavened bread or any food containing yeast, and all traces are removed. For one week, *matzoth* (unleavened bread) and various pancakes and puddings made of unleavened ingredients replace all bread products on the menu.

Highlight of the Passover celebration is the *Seder* service—a family banquet held on the first and second evenings of Passover (Reform Jews have one *Seder*). The *Seder* is an elaborate ritual. The table is decorated with fruits and flowers, the best china and candlesticks, and other marks of festivity. A wine cup beside each place setting is used for the four sips of wine—symbol of joy.

Essentially the ceremony consists of telling the story of the Exodus, using various symbols for illustration and dramatization. The youngest child at the table asks four questions of his father: "Why is this night different from all other nights of the year: (1) in regard to the eating of unleavened bread, (2) the use of bitter herbs, (3) the ritual of dipping food in salt water, and (4) the custom of leaning at the *Seder* table?" The story the father unfolds, read from a book known as the *Haggadah*, is the familiar tale of Egyptian slavery, Pharaoh's obstinate refusal to let the Israelites go, Moses' courageous leadership and the miracle of redemption.

Various items of food each have their lesson: the hard-boiled egg is the symbol of life—Israel's optimistic affirmation of the sanctity of life. It is dipped in salt water in sympathy with the bitter lot of our ancestors. For the same reason, bitter herbs are eaten. A mixture of nuts and apples reminds the family of the mortar used by the Hebrew slaves in building cities for the cruel taskmasters.

The father sits at the head of the table, leaning on a pillow, Oriental fashion, to signify a feeling of leisure.

An important part of the Passover is the tradition that our blessings are to be shared with the less fortunate. The Cup of Elijah is filled, the front door is opened, and the family waits in silence while the spirit of the prophet Elijah, symbol of the humble wayfarer, enters to share in the *Seder*.

Custom dictates that guests be invited to the family table. In addition to friends, a student away from home, a soldier or any traveler far from his family are welcome visitors.

The festival is commemorated with special synagogue worship: the Torah is read, recounting the narrative of the Exodus, and *Hallel*, the psalms of praise are chanted.

An interesting sidelight is the tradition of reciting only part of the *Hallel* during most of Passover. This practice goes back to an ancient legend which tells that when the Israelites crossed the Red Sea they chanted songs of praise for their deliverance. A voice from On High spoke out: "You must not sing songs of gladness when my creatures, the Egyptians, have drowned in the sea." In sympathy for Israel's fallen enemies, the songs that are chanted on other festive days are omitted for six days of the Passover week.

The feast of Passover has become the symbol of one of mankind's most cherished ideals—freedom from enslavement. To the Jew, it is an annual reminder that the work of freedom is never ended. "In each generation, the Jew must regard himself as though he personally had been delivered from the hands of the Egyptians," declares the *Haggadah*.

The modern State of Israel has, understandably, taken the festival of Passover especially to its heart. To hundreds of thousands of its citizens, the epic of Egyptian bondage has been relived in concentration camps and displaced persons' shelters. The new Promised Land, on the very soil of the old, is a reality which lends both poignancy and exultation to the Israeli celebration of the Feast of Liberation.

Shevuoth

SHEVUOTH is the Festival of Weeks, or Pentecost, which is celebrated in late May or early June, exactly seven weeks after the Feast of Passover. Unlike the other major feasts, it is observed for only two days (only one in the Reform).

Originally Shevuoth was an agricultural festival—the Feast of First Fruits. But during the years the holiday has been endowed with another meaning—the anniversary of the giving of the Law.

The Book of Exodus is read on Shevuoth, including the chapter containing the Ten Commandments. The general theme of the day is our traditional love of learning. The Book of Ruth, the delightful story of a Moabite girl's devotion to the faith of her adoption, is also read in the synagogue on the Feast of Weeks.

The synagogue is decorated with various fresh fruits in remembrance of the ceremony of Temple days, when offerings of first fruits were carried by the pilgrims to Jerusalem. In modern Israel, the custom is observed by farmers from all parts of the land who meet in the city of Haifa and take part in a procession carrying baskets of freshly gathered fruits.

In recent years, Shevuoth has also become the festival of Confirmation in both the Reform and Conservative ritual.

Minor Fasts and Feasts

IN ADDITION to the major religious days in the Jewish calendar, Orthodox Jews observe two traditional periods of mourning commemorating ancient disasters. One is the Sefirah, the six weeks immediately following Passover. In remembrance of the Roman persecutions, and the martyrdom of such rabbis as Akiba, no weddings or other festive affairs are scheduled during this period.

Another three-week period of mourning is observed every summer in commemoration of the destruction of the ancient Temple and Jerusalem. This season is climaxed by a Fast Day called the Ninth of Ab (the Hebrew date), when special synagogue services are held and the Book of Lamentations is read in a plaintive minor key. The same sad melody is used in the services on the Sabbath preceding the Fast. The following Sabbath is called the Sabbath of Consolation. The synagogue is decked in white and the congregation reads the 40th chapter of Isaiah: "Comfort ye, comfort ye, My people."

Tu Bishvat, the Jewish Arbor Day, usually falls in February and marks the tree planting season of ancient Israel. Custom dictates that fruits distinctive to Israel be eaten, among them St. John's bread. In modern Israel, school children, each bearing a young sapling, take part in a ceremonial planting of trees. Because reforestation is an important Israeli goal, the annual planting ceremonies have become very festive occasions.

Each new day of the Hebrew month (Rosh Hodesh), is a semi-holiday on which the new moon is greeted with special religious ceremonial. In ancient times no work was done on Rosh Hodesh. Later it developed into a woman's holiday; once a month the housewife was freed completely from her regular duties. According to legend, this was to reward the women for refusing to join their menfolk in worship of the golden calf while Moses was on Mount Sinai receiving the Law.

Today, this custom has disappeared, although a campaign for its revival would probably elicit enthusiastic feminine support.

VII

MODERN ISRAEL

*The world will be freed by our liberty,
enriched by our wealth, magnified by our
greatness. And whatever we attempt there
to accomplish for our own welfare, will
react powerfully and beneficially for the
good of humanity.*

THEODOR HERZL, *The Jewish State*

Modern Israel

DURING the summer of 1936 I was traveling on the Adriatic Sea on my way from Palestine to Trieste. The breathless beauty of the Dalmatian coast was the subject of shipboard comment all day. One fellow passenger, an Austrian Jew returning from an extended visit to Palestine, muttered protestingly: "Why didn't the Almighty choose this place instead of that desolate spot in Asia to give us the Ten Commandments?"

The words were spoken half in jest. He was complaining against history, but he realized that its course was inexorable—Palestine was the Promised Land and not the Adriatic. And though he didn't know it then, Jewish labors and devotion were to make of "that desolate spot in Asia" a garden spot in the Middle East.

At the turn of the twentieth century only five thousand new Jewish settlers had established themselves on the soil of the Holy Land. And until the rise of Hitlerism their numbers increased very slowly. Even after 1933 the British permitted only a few hundred immigrants each year, though additional thousands poured in illegally, despite a formidable blockade.

As the incredible reports of what was happenings to Jews in German concentration camps began to come through, the campaign for the re-establishment of the Jewish homeland took on a new urgency, not so much as a fulfillment of the biblical prophecy, as a haven for the pitifully few who escaped the gas chambers and the crematoriums.

The United Nations creation of the independent State of Israel, in May, 1948, was hailed by Jews throughout the world, regardless of their attitude towards Zionism. Even behind the Iron Curtain, the visit of the first envoy from Israel to Moscow occasioned a hysterical outburst of enthusiasm among Russian Jews. Only a minor segment of Jews continued their opposition to the new state after it had been recognized by the United Nations.

On the other hand, the Arab world has always resisted Jewish immigration into Palestine. The Promised Land, they declared, had been promised to them at the very time that the British government, through the Balfour Declaration, had assured the Jewish right to create a homeland in Palestine.

It is hardly the scope of this book to weigh the merits of the conflicting views—nor does this author claim a completely unbiased position. Various impartial commissions, representing many different countries, have passed judgment on the rival claims; and the United Nations acted on the findings of its Special Committee on Palestine to establish the new state.

The Christian world has naturally maintained a lively interest in developments in the Holy Land, for Israel's soil holds sacred memories for all Christians. The names of towns and regions that appear in the daily press are as familiar to the devout Christian as the Bible. Nazareth, the Sea of Galilee, Megiddo (the ancient Armageddon) all arouse deep religious associations for him. And the streets of Jerusalem, its gates and its byways are intimate reminders of the teacher who came down from Galilee and founded a new faith. Thus, for Jew, Moslem and Christian alike, the little State of Israel will always continue to have a magnetic attraction.

A visitor to the new State may be disappointed on his immediate arrival. The residents of Israel seem unaware of their special role in the drama the whole world is watching. Despite my frequent visits to Israel, I am constantly surprised by the similarities to our own normal routines of living. A crowded bus, taking people to work, stops at a filling station. As the attendant fills the tank, he hums along with the music of Beethoven's 9th Symphony blaring forth from a radio in the garage.

Children play with the same accents of unrestraint that mark children everywhere. From the mills of a huge factory, miles of paper roll off the machinery. In the countryside, families till the land with tractors marked "International Harvester," just like families in Kansas and Michigan.

In this very "normalcy" of Israeli life is the true miracle. For in this land as old as the Bible, people snatched from death have built a modern, fruitful, democratic nation in a few short years.

Many signs of newness are apparent. The Hadassah organization, reflecting the energies of American women who have raised millions of dollars for the health and youth of Israel, has erected and equipped a new Medical Center that is destined to be a shrine of healing and learning in that part of the world.

The great Weizmann Institute, to my mind one of the beauty spots in the world, and the Haifa Technion, Israel's major engineering school, are models for modern scientific research. But even more astounding than the physical growth of the nation is the spirit and energy of its citizens, so ably described by Dr. Garcia-Granados, Guatemalan representative on the United Nations Palestine Commission:

> This is really a fascinating country, a melting pot for the Jews of the whole world. The curious thing is that although they bring with them widely different customs,

they become assimilated in no time.... In the briefest time, blonds of the north become indistinguishable from the Spanish-speaking Sephardim. ... Trying to analyze what it is they express, what it is that steels them to meet the future, I think it is this: a single-minded determination and singleness of purpose; a patriotic group fervor, which makes them almost supermen in their capacity to work and endure hardship; an energy so tremendous that they have been able, for example, to revive Hebrew, a dead tongue, and make it a national language spoken perfectly by children and old men. ... All I can say is that thanks to their will, their determination, their virtual dedication to the job before them, they are converting Palestine into one of the most progressive countries in the world.

Is Zionism a Religious or a Political Movement?

ZIONISM is both a religious and a political movement. As part of their faith Jews have prayed ceaselessly for the rebirth of their homeland. Three times a day in worship, the observant ask God to rebuild Zion. In the marriage ceremony, in the mourning ritual, at the Passover *Seder*, the hope for a Jewish state is expressed, even by those who were never political Zionists.

Politically, Zionism is a movement to re-establish the Jews as a people in the land of Israel. A Zionist believes that such a homeland will secure the welfare of Jews throughout the world, and serve as a source of spiritual and cultural inspiration to the Jews of all lands. The Zionist hopes that a nation built on the principles of social justice laid down in Jewish tradition will become a model of a high ethical order that will teach mankind anew the moral teachings of the Hebrew prophets.

The political efforts which led to the creation of the new Jewish State began about sixty years ago. Since the middle of the nineteenth century, Jews of Eastern Europe living under the rigors of Czarist tyranny saw in Palestine the only answer to the age-old problem of homelessness.

At first the Jews of Western Europe had little sympathy for the idea. But when they discovered that emancipation had not rooted out the evil of anti-Semitism, many were disillusioned, and gathered around a young Viennese journalist, Doctor Theodor Herzl, who is considered the father of Zionism. The official Zionist movement was formally organized in 1897. Although its followers were united in general purpose, they differed in their specific interests. Some felt that Palestine was a refuge for the oppressed; others hoped that it would bring a rebirth of Jewish culture and the Hebrew language. Religious Jews believed that in a homeland of their own they could adhere to the rituals of their faith more fully; still others saw in Zionism a safeguard against assimilation.

The Orthodox were not all agreed on Zionism either. One segment clung to the belief that only a Messiah could redeem Israel. But the vast majority found in the movement for revival a fulfillment of biblical dreams and of their daily prayers.

There are, of course, many shades of opinion among Jews today regarding Zionism. At one extreme, there are those who interpret it to mean the "ingathering of the exiles"—the return of all Jews to Israel. Quite naturally, this view has its strongest adherents in those lands where life is intolerable for Jews. In the United States, on the other hand, even the leaders of Zionism reject this idea and only a minute percentage of American Jews have emigrated to Israel.

At the other extreme, there are anti-Zionists—those Jews who are opposed to the creation of a Jewish State because they feel this threatens the position of Jews in other lands.

Between the extremes, there are those who look upon Israel as a haven for the persecuted and a beacon of democratic light in the Near East, but continue to consider themselves an integral part of the lands in which they live (see p. 190).

Why Does Israel Welcome So Many Immigrants?

IN THE harbor at Haifa, Israel, an old steamer rests at anchor. It has outlived its usefulness, but despite the crowded port, the ship has been left there as an historic symbol—a monument to homelessness.

The vessel is the famous ship, the Exodus, which in 1947 carried a load of refugees from Europe to Palestine—only to be turned back by the British authorities and forced to take its hapless human cargo to a port in Germany. The Exodus is also a reminder of other vessels, such as the ill-fated Patria and the Struma, which plunged to the bottom of the sea with their human cargoes of men, women and children—all refugees without a port.

The tragedies of the 1940's were a repetition of history. In the 1490's, too, thousands of Jews fleeing from the Inquisition perished in the depths of the sea or in killing treks from one land to another.

These experiences have made Jews allergic to immigration quotas and border restrictions. When the State of Israel was created, all barriers were removed, even though it was economically unsound to absorb as many immigrants as there were inhabitants. Not only were the doors opened wide, but the citizens of Israel imposed heavy taxes upon themselves to pay for transporting immigrants *into* their land.

Israel's immigration policy has also been determined by the practices of other countries. The virtual closing of gates in most of the democratic world meant that the refugees could either go to Israel—or nowhere. Above and beyond all political considerations are the human ones. Israel's policy of free immigration is a reflection of a people moved to compassion for their suffering brothers. The individual citizens of Israel do not complain about the hardships brought about by sharing their food, their homes, their meager resources with new immigrants who bring nothing with them but their unhappy memories. The insistent demands of Soviet Jewry evoke an automatic response in Israelis. They are their brothers' keepers."

In addition, though most people do not think of Israel as a frontier country, a visitor's first reaction is that Israel is largely a land of empty space.

The outlying agricultural communities on the borders of Lebanon, Syria and Jordan, frequently have no more than a hundred settlers. They face the normal hazards of frontier life —and the hostility of neighboring states who have yet to make peace with them. If these inhabitants number two hundred instead of one hundred their safety and the security of these colonies is immeasurably strengthened.

Aside from these reasons, the basic answer to Israel's open

door policy lies in its philosophy of Jewish life. The citizens of Israel believe that every Jew who wants to settle in the new State has an inalienable, God-given right to do so. They can no more deny him the right of entrance to his land than they would bar his entry to his house of worship.

Is the Religion of Israel More Orthodox Than in Other Parts of the World?

A LARGE majority of Israelis are not Orthodox. The individual observance of religious ritual, such as the dietary laws and strict adherence to the Sabbath laws, is no more noticeable in Israel than in any other country.

Jerusalem, however, is the exception in this respect. For centuries pious Jews have come to the Holy City for prayer, study and meditation. And today in Jerusalem there are scores of congregations of the pious, whose lives are devoted to little besides worship and study of the *Torah*. Youngsters with earlocks, wearing frock coats and caftans, are a common sight in the streets of Jerusalem. But they are a rarity in the rest of the land. The remnants of Jewish mysticism are to be found in these Orthodox circles, in Jerusalem and in the city of Safed.

The cultural melting pot of Israel is to be found in the army and navy. The compulsory military training law has brought the extremely Orthodox young people into the armed services, where social pressure usually convinces most of them to give up their earlocks. It is fairly safe to predict that the visible signs of extreme Orthodoxy will ultimately vanish, even in Jerusalem.

As for the average Israeli in Tel Aviv or Haifa, the pattern of religious observance varies little from that of other lands.

Is the State of Israel Controlled by Religious Authority?

THE modern State of Israel is not a theocracy—it is not governed by the rabbinate of Jerusalem or any other religious leaders. Its government is democratically elected by all the citizens (including non-Jews) and represents the political will of the population.

Rabbi Emanuel Rackman, a leading authority on Jewish law, tells us that in the light of history and "the literature regarded by pious Jews as authentic . . . the separation of church and state is a Jewish point of view. Judaism did not want persons vested with priestly powers to possess political powers at the same time."

The laws of the new State are civil laws, except those that govern marriage and the family. Israel has an "established church" comparable to the Church of England. Like the Archbishop of Canterbury, the Chief Rabbi has a legal status in Jewish religious matters, but his influence on the conduct of government is nominal.

Since the overwhelming majority of Israel's citizens are Jewish, such institutions as the Sabbath and the festivals are an integral part of community life. But each person is free to decide for himself how to observe these days.

There is no religious test for office—a prime minister or a cabinet member may be a synagogue-goer, or he may not. Several delegates to the Knesset (Parliament) are Arabs.

The one serious source of friction between the civil and religious leaders has been the matter of religion in public life. The rabbis insisted—and the government unwillingly agreed—that on the Sabbath, the nation's official day of rest, public conveyances would be restricted, dietary laws would be observed in all state institutions including the armed forces.

Those who support these state-buttressed religious observances believe that the system preserves the rights of religious conscience. An Orthodox youth who is drafted into the Army, they argue, has the right to follow his religious principles in the matter of diet. Therefore the kosher laws must apply to army food. Similarly, the strict Sabbath enforcement, it is claimed, will not interfere with the non-observant, but will insure full freedom of conscience to the Orthodox.

Those who oppose government backing for religious ritual are less concerned with principle than with practical considerations. The curtailing of bus service on the only day of the week when workers can travel to see relatives and friends, or when they can escape from the summer's heat at the beach, arouses deep resentment on the part of most Israelis.

Some visitors to Israel deplore the preference given to Orthodoxy over other, liberal, forms of worship and practice. But actually, few non-Orthodox religious movements exist in the country, so it is not really a question of favoring one group more than another.

The form of religious expression now found in Israel is an extremely narrow interpretation of Jewish tradition. No sermons are preached in the synagogues of Jerusalem. The functions of the rabbis are almost exclusively ritual. A chaplain of an Israeli hospital does not visit the patients, he supervises the kitchen to check on its adherence to the kosher laws. This rigid view of religion has divided the Israelis into two camps—the extremely Orthodox and those who are entirely indifferent to religion. It is to be hoped that after the "frontier stage" of Israel's history is over, a broader interpretation of religion will develop, one that is more in consonance with the traditional spirit of Judaism. Such a development will, no doubt, lead to a head-on clash between the Orthodox group and the rest of the population, which will probably result in the separation of institutional religion and the state. In my opinion, both Judaism and the state will be richer for it.

This does not mean that Israel will not always retain a distinct religious quality. For as ancient tradition says, "The land of Israel is inseparable from the religion of Israel."

The teachings of Moses, Isaiah, Rabbi Akiba and Moses Maimonides, it is hoped, will continue to be the cornerstone of Israel's culture as they have been the cornerstone of Judaism's proud heritage through the centuries.

What Is the Status of Christians and Moslems in Modern Israel?

CLOSE to a half-million Christians and Moslems live in Israel and they have full citizenship rights.

A simple barometer of relative freedom in two areas is an

examination of the traffic pattern between those areas. In 1967, many Arabs fled from the occupied West bank of Jordan, but as they began to feel more secure the flow was reversed. In addition, each summer close to 200,000 tourists from all Arab lands visit the West bank and have access to all the tourist places in Israel, hardly an indication of tension between Arab and Jew.

Immediately after the creation of the new State of Israel the government appointed a Minister of Religious Affairs whose sole duty is to protect and guarantee the rights of religious minorities—a unique institution among the countries of the world. A Department of Christian Affairs, for example, watches over the welfare of all Christian churches. I noticed that at every church entrance a sign in three languages warned against any intrusion by non-Christians. In order to gain entrance, even as a tourist, I had to obtain special permission.

The values which are generally prized, education, health, and economic well-being, are nourished for the Arab minority in Israel as well as the occupied territories. In the month following the 1967 war, a Jerusalem Arab family visiting Jewish neighbors with whom they had been reunited after a 19-year separation confided to them that their bright teen-age son would now be able to attend "your university—we mean *our* university now that Jerusalem is one city." That same month a Bethlehem Christian Arab brought his wife, who had been declared a terminal case, to the Hadassah Hospital in Jerusalem, and happily discovered that a recent research breakthrough would enable the physicians to cure her. A stonemason from Ramallah met his brother in Haifa, engaged in the same work he had done in Jordan, only to discover that in contrast to his modest status, his Israeli brother owned his own home and automobile.

The Israeli law covering compulsory education is a great

novelty in the Near East. Less than half the children in the Arab world see the inside of a High School. In 1948 only 11,000 Palestine Arab children were enrolled in school; in 1971 there were over 110,000. No more than 15% of the girls attended classes when the State of Israel was born, female enrollment now approximates the proportion of male students. About one third of Arab children between 14 and 17 now attend school. One tenth of the University of Haifa students are Arabs.

Under British rule in Palestine, Arab government workers were paid less for the same work than Christians and Jewish employees. One of the first acts of the new State was to wipe out this differential, so that the Arabs would be able to raise their living standards to those of their neighbors. But perhaps most important of all is the complete political equality which the Arabs enjoy. The Arab delegates in the Knesset were elected, as were all the legislators, by Moslem, Jewish and Christian alike. The sight of these turbaned delegates, when I visited the Knesset, brought home to me the firmly rooted tradition in Judaism of dealing with all men fairly. "Remember ye were slaves in the land of Egypt," says the Bible. And modern Israel has not forgotten.

How Do the Israeli 'Collectives' Operate?

OVER forty years ago a few dozen hardy pioneers laid the foundations for the modern State of Israel with a group of co-operative agricultural settlements known as *kibbutzim*. A *kibbutz* is a farm colony which is run on a share-and-share-alike basis. It is quite similar to the Christian socialist settlements established in the United States during the nineteenth century, or some of the Amish and Mennonite communities. All share equally in the work according to their individual talents and capacities; and all receive an equal share of the benefits. The tradition goes back to the Bible, which declares that all property belongs to God, and man is only His trustee.

The *kibbutzim* performed a vitally important function in the early years of colonization in Israel. Life was very austere, and the *halutz* or pioneer, could look forward to little beyond a minimum of economic security and the peace of mind which comes from seeing the fruits of toil and sacrifice. Only hardy spirits, fired by idealism, would undertake this kind of life. And it was this idealism which made possible the completely cooperative living of the *kibbutz*.

The *kibbutz* is not a commune in the Soviet sense. It is one of several different kinds of farm communities in Israel. And there is no compulsion about joining or staying on the *kibbutz*. Many who find this form of group life unappealing leave for neighboring free enterprise settlements, or for city life.

The *kibbutzim* are governed by leaders democratically elected by the membership. There is no centralized authority over all the *kibbutzim*; each group determines its own destiny.

After the State of Israel was established, the agricultural cooperatives declined in importance. The State undertook an ambitious program of land development and there was much less incentive for groups of young people to form their own *kibbutz*. The newcomers from Europe, and particularly from the Oriental countries, had little appetite for "covered wagon" life. In the first two years of the State, when its population grew sixty-six per cent, the collectives grew only twenty per cent. At present less than six per cent of the Israelis live in the collectives.

The *kibbutzim* I visited in the summer of 1952 were much different from those I had seen on previous visits. Their idealism was as fervent as ever, but life was more comfortable in all but the newest settlements. And the extremes of collective life had been modified. For example, individuals are permitted their own personal allowances to spend as they see fit. I asked one of the leaders whether his wrist watch belonged to him. Yes, it had come out of savings. But repairs to the watch were the responsibility of the group. "What about saving money to bring in relatives still left in Europe?" I asked. That, too, was a group responsibility. If the members of the *kibbutz* approved of such a request, they would subsidize immigration together.

Today, the collectives are more than agricultural communities. They also manufacture a good many products, especially those needed on farms, such as irrigation sprinklers, tiles, faucets, drums to carry oil and scores of other necessities. Some of the machinery I saw could be compared to that of Milwaukee, Wisconsin or Moline, Illinois. (As a matter of fact, the names of Wisconsin, Minnesota and Illinois are quite commonplace on the farms of Israel.)

But even industrialization has not watered down the idealism of the pioneers who are attempting to fashion a community based on the social principles of the ancient prophets.

In Lower Galilee I watched a group of young adults building a school for their youngsters. The oldest child in the colony was four, and there was only a year in which to complete the building for the primary group. Every stone in the school, every piece of cement tubing bringing water to the building, the faucets, the chairs, tables, benches, blackboard, grew out of the labors of the parents.

As Israel becomes increasingly urban, the collectives, which a generation ago were the backbone of Jewish life in Palestine, assume a more modest place in the economy of the land. But they have already contributed much to the spiritual character of its people. The dignity of labor and the willingness to sacrifice the comforts of the present for the future, are dominant characteristics of the Israeli's way of life.

Does Israel Hope to Expand Its Territory?

JUDGED by American standards Israel is a tiny country, but the people and their government seem to be much more interested in the amount of room they already have for immigrants than in campaigning for more space. Except for a tiny minority of extremists, there is no talk of expansion in newspapers, public statements or street conversation.

Israel's physical contour is bizarre—two wide expanses of land joined by a narrow strip along the Mediterranean coast. In the trains when traveling through the bottleneck part of the country, the story goes that one sees signs quipping, "Please do not lean out of the State."

Despite this handicap, the overwhelming majority of the people of Israel seem to have no desire to widen their boundaries. Plans for the future center on improving the quality of the soil they now possess—by erosion control, soil chemistry and mechanized farming. There is little interest in quantity. In the words of Professor Heschel, Judaism has always been more concerned with Time than with Space.

What Form of Government Does
Israel Have?

ISRAEL is part of the family of democratic nations. Its government structure is close to the British or French parliamentary system, with supreme authority vested in the Knesset, a body of representatives elected by the people.

Like France, too, Israel has a number of political parties, rather than the two major parties of the American system. The religious bloc consists of several parties; labor is represented by two major parties, one of which, the Mapai (moderate socialist) is in power. Mapam, the other labor party, is more radical in its outlook. (The two names are made up of the initials of two workers' organizations.) The conservative view is represented by the General Zionists and the Progressive Party. Two other groups, the nationalists (Herut) and the Communists, have a combined following of less than five per cent of the population. Both are vocal but without real influence. Many Israeli Arabs belong to the Communist Party and two of the three Arab representatives in the Knesset are Communist. The number of parliamentary seats held by each of the political parties is based on the proportion of votes that party received at the polls. The Presidency of Israel, like that of France, is an honorary office, bestowed upon a beloved elder statesman.

Political feelings run high in Israel. Youngsters develop

partisan alignments early, with a good deal of fervor and fanat-
icism. Every shade of political opinion enjoys full freedom of
speech, press and assembly, and the Israeli electorate is one of
the best informed in the world on the issues before them.

Over seventy per cent of those eligible vote in elections, and
in 1949, Arab women voted for the first time in Palestine history. Thus, Israel well deserves the title of democratic bastion
in the Middle East.

Is an American Jew's First Loyalty to Israel or America?

THE only loyalty of an American Jew is to the United
States of America—without any ifs, ands or buts. To the Jew,
the State of Israel is the ancestral home of his forefathers, the
birthplace of his faith and his Bible. He recalls with pride that
it was this land which gave the western world its religious traditions and its moral law. To the Christian and the Moslem it is
the Holy Land. But its holiness grew out of Jewish prophets,
Jewish teachers, Jewish writings.

Israel is the haven for over three million Jews—after the ago-
nies and nightmare and murders of the past thirty years. Surely,
it is not surprising that Israel has great and special meaning for
Jews all over the world. Nor is it surprising that the courage
and the pioneering of the people of Israel have won the respect
of men of every religious faith.

But spiritual bonds and emotional ties are quite different
from political loyalty. American Jews will continue to watch

the development of the new State with sentimental interest, and to offer moral and material aid to it. Many Americans retain strong attachments to the land of their fathers. But their political loyalty—whether they be Irish, German or Italian; Catholic, Protestant or Jew—is and will always be to America alone.

Does Israel's New Status as a Modern State Weaken Its Biblical Role?

THE creation of a modern state, with all its apparatus of government, may seem quite remote from the prophetic vision of a land destined as "a light unto the nations." Yet, the forces of contemporary history have lent a measure of reality to the dreams of Isaiah and Ezekiel. Already there is a generous flow of technical help from Israel to the even younger states of Ghana, Burma and Nigeria, offering the infant African countries the benefits of Israel's experience in government, health and welfare, and scientific education.

The resurgence of a Jewish consciousness among the Jews of the Soviet Union partakes of the quality of a biblical miracle. I would have predicted, when I visited Russia in 1956, that the young Jews of that country were permanently lost. Yet somehow a spark has been kindled among tens of thousands utterly removed from any Judaic exposure that has impelled them to renew their identity with the people of Israel at tremendous personal risk. "Out of Zion shall go forth the Law, and the word of the Lord out of Jerusalem," said the prophets.

VIII

JEWS AND CHRISTIANS

I call heaven and earth to witness that whether it be Gentile or Israelite, man or woman, slave or handmaid, according to the deeds which he does, so will the Holy Spirit rest on him.

THE *Talmud*

Jews and Christians

In the days of Charlemagne a group of Jews settled in the southern part of France, finding peace and security as tillers of the land. Pope Stephen III marked the occasion in a noteworthy epistle to the Bishop of Narbonne: "With deep regret and mortal anxiety we have heard from you that the Jewish people are on Christian soil and in enjoyment of full equality with Christians."

This was Jewry's first unhappy introduction to the Christian world. In the succeeding centuries the Jews of Europe and the Americas were destined to remain a minority group in a civilization that was predominantly Christian. It was not a happy world for any religious minority: the Protestants in France, the Catholics in early New Amsterdam, the dissident followers of Roger Williams in Massachusetts, the non-conformists in Calvin's Geneva. For a dozen centuries Jews suffered every kind of persecution, ranging from unimportant social slurs to the tortures of the rack.

Jews, in turn, built an emotional barrier between themselves and the Christian community. Even if the gates were open, they preferred not to venture out into the "Gentile" world.

A few shafts of light did burst through the darkness: the Catholic Abbés, Grégoire and Maury, and the Protestant pastor, Rabaut-Saint-Étienne, who fought for equal rights for

Jews in the eighteenth century; Thomas Macaulay, whose brilliant oratory moved England to acts of tolerance; and others, rare but spirited, whose passion for humanity outweighed the narrower dogmas of creed. But a realistic approach to an understanding of Jewish-Christian relations must bear in mind those thousand years of conflict.

Today, in the United States, we have begun to create a single community of Christians and Jews based on mutual respect and understanding. Nevertheless, group memories run deep. The centuries of Christian teaching that the Jews are despised because they rejected the Savior, himself a Jew; and of Jewish suspicion of Gentiles, and fear of them, are not easily wiped out in the minds of either Christian or Jew. We have much to unlearn of hate before the vital lessons of love and amity can fully penetrate.

American educators, religious leaders and others who are trying to overcome the past and build a better future, have given much thought to the problem of Jewish-Christian relations. And in the past decade, particularly, we have matured in our grasp of both the problem and the solution.

There was a time when it was thought that the most important thing was to portray the minority group in a good light. Scores of books were written on the subject of Jewish contributions to civilization; Jewish efforts in American wars; the great Jewish scientists and medical researchers. But modern insights have made us realize that group tensions are not eased merely by impressing one group with the virtues of the other. When I read *One Foot in Heaven*, a book about a Methodist minister's family in Iowa, I was particularly intrigued by the amusing accounts of petty squabbles in an average Methodist congregation. They were rather like the controversies one might hear within the family of synagogue life! My estimate of Methodists did not fall because I discovered these imperfections. On the contrary, it was good to know that these fine people, "made in the image of God," were also made in the likeness of man, with all his foibles and shortcomings.

Recently, while lecturing in Dallas, Texas, I told an audience of Christians and Jews that I had just conducted a Passover service in Sing Sing Prison, and that it had been a very moving experience. I added that a decade ago many Jews would have hesitated to tell non-Jews the sad truth that some of our co-religionists were behind prison bars. After the lecture, a gentleman came forward, grasped my hand and introduced himself. As a Catholic, he said, he was most impressed with my remarks about Sing Sing. He had always thought that only his core-ligionists got into that kind of trouble!

A number of factors must be credited for the growing improvement in Jewish-Christian relations over the years. First, is the American public school system, possibly the single most potent influence for intergroup amity. A child who attends our public schools learns the sanctity of the individual and respect for human rights as part of his natural heritage. He is taught to reject racial and religious bigotry as unworthy of his better self and to view suspiciously the hatemonger and the pied piper of prejudice. Above all, he is impressed with the urgency that all Americans learn to live together in harmony and mutual respect for one another.

In addition, the work of such educational forces as Jewish and interfaith community relations organizations, the social action bodies of the Catholic and Protestant churches, the various women's organizations and other community and civic groups, have done much to raise the level of Jewish-Christian harmony.

And not to be overlooked is the experience of World War

II, when the bulk of American youth shared in the common cause of their country's defense. Eleven million young men and seven thousand priests, ministers and rabbis whose previous contacts with one another had been most casual, found themselves in the same foxholes, the same chapels, the same dangers. It would be inconceivable if a common ground of humanity did not develop out of this intimate association.

Thus, in the past decade, the phrase *Judaeo-Christian heritage* has gained popular currency. It was born out of the realization that the differences which divide Jews and Christians are not as significant as the ideals they cherish together. It reflects also a *creative partnership*, a recognition that Jews and Christians can reach a firm basis of understanding and mutual respect *without* yielding on matters of principle; and that Jews do not have to forswear their religious and cultural uniqueness in order to accommodate themselves to a preponderantly Christian society.

With the challenge of fascism and naziism in the 1930's and 40's, and the more recent menace of communism, the phrase Judaeo-Christian heritage has given birth to a consciousness of common destiny as well as common past. The spiritual approach to life, with its concern for the sanctity of the individual, has been threatened by the cynical ruthlessness of the authoritarian regimes. In face of these dangers, Christians and Jews see a crucial necessity to unite their strength to preserve their precious values.

The tensions in the Near East and the plight of Soviet Jewry have sometimes produced frustrations among Jews because of seeming Christian apathy, and a feeling of disappointment among Christians because of what they regard as Jewish stubbornness. But the lines of communication have been generally firm, and have moved in a constructive direction.

Do Christianity and Judaism Agree on Anything? On What Points Do They Differ?

CHRISTIANS and Jews share the same rich heritage of the Old Testament, with its timeless truths and its unchanging values. They share their belief in the fatherhood of one God, all-knowing, all-powerful, ever-merciful, the God of Abraham, Isaac and Jacob. They share their faith in the sanctity of the Ten Commandments, the wisdom of the prophets and the brotherhood of man. Central to both faiths is the firm belief in the spirit of man; in the pursuit of peace and the hatred of war; in the democratic ideal as a guide to the political and social order; and, above all, in the imperishable nature of man's soul.

Christian and Jew both believe that man was placed on this world for a purpose—that life is far more than "a brilliant interlude between two nothings." The social goal of Christianity and Judaism is also one: a world that is motivated by love, understanding and consideration for our fellow men.

These are the basic points of agreement—the broad common ground of Judaism and Christianity that makes up the Judaeo-Christian heritage. For the roots of Christianity run deeply into the soil of Judaism, the Old Testament and the Moral Law.

And the common inheritance of both faiths has laid the groundwork for much that we know as western civilization.

Two centuries ago, a German dramatist, Gotthold Ephraim Lessing, caught the essence of this common heritage in a play called *Nathan, the Wise*. One of the most memorable scenes depicts a meeting between a friar and the Jew, Nathan. The friar, moved by the beauty of Nathan's character, cries out: "Nathan! Nathan! You are a Christian! By God, you are a Christian! There never was a better Christian!" His friend replies: "We are of one mind! *For that which makes me, in your eyes, a Christian, makes you, in my eyes, a Jew!*"

But there are, of course, many areas of disagreement between the two religions. Jews do not accept the divinity of Jesus as the "only begotten Son" of God. We recognize him as a child of God only in the sense that we are all God's children, for the ancient rabbis taught us that one of God's greatest gifts to man is the knowledge that we are made in His image.

Jews also reject the principle of incarnation—God becoming flesh. It is a cardinal tenet of our faith that God is purely spiritual and admits of no human attributes. Nor can Judaism accept the principle of vicarious atonement—the idea of salvation through Christ. We cannot, therefore, recognize a relationship between an act of self-sacrifice in ancient Palestine and our own deliverance. No one, we believe, can serve as an intermediary between man and God, even in a symbolic sense. We approach God—each man after his own fashion—without a mediator.

Judaism also differs with Christianity on the doctrine of original sin. We do not interpret the story of Adam and Eve as reflecting man's fall from grace. Unlike Christianity, we have made no attempt to derive from the Garden of Eden allegory any lessons or rules about the nature of man.

These are some of the major differences of doctrine between Judaism and Christianity. There are others as well. But to enumerate them all is neither possible nor necessary in a book of this nature.

Are Jews Forbidden to Read the New Testament?

THE phrase, "forbidden to read" is entirely alien to Judaism. No authority would dare suggest that a mature human being be "forbidden to read" anything. (See "Censorship," p. 41.) There has certainly never been a ban against reading the Gospels or other Christian writings.

However, the synagogue makes no effort to encourage the reading of the New Testament since it has no *religious* connotation in Jewish life. Nor will a quotation from the Gospels be heard from the pulpit of an Orthodox synagogue for the same reason.

The generations of Jews who suffered humiliation and persecution in the Spanish Inquisition or in Church-inspired Polish pogroms quite naturally discouraged their children from reading the Christian Bible. They had no way of knowing that it contained words about peace and brotherhood.

But in modern times such antipathy is rapidly diminishing. I have seen pious Jews poring over the contents of missionary literature and many Jewish scholars know the Gospels as intimately as the Old Testament which is the basis for our creed.

Students preparing for the rabbinate often use the New Testament in their studies. A serious student finds the New

Testament indispensable to a full understanding of Jewish history of the early Christian era.

A number of rabbis take their graduate work at Christian theological schools. In recent years, scores of Christian seminaries, Protestant and Catholic, have named rabbis and Jewish scholars to their faculties.

Most Jewish educators, however, disapprove of teaching *about* Christianity in synagogue schools since they do not feel that it is the duty of a religious school to teach its students the tenets and history of other faiths. But many liberal synagogues offer courses for post-confirmation students and adults in which all the major religions are discussed. A modern curriculum would normally take into account the basic fact that Jewish children ought to be informed about the Christian culture in which they will be practicing their own faith, and will find valuable guidance in such textbooks as "The Jew and His Christian Neighbor."

Do Jews Try to Convert Gentiles?

MODERN Judaism is not a proselytizing religious creed, though there was a time when Jews did engage in an active missionary program. During Roman rule, many Roman noblemen and their wives were attracted to the teachings of the rabbis. And in many remote parts of the world today, the existence of devout Jewish tribes, distantly removed from the birthplace of Judaism, gives evidence of earlier Jewish missionary work, so far back in antiquity that its origins cannot be traced. In southeastern Russia an entire nation called the Chazars were inducted into Judaism because their monarch was won over to its teachings. There is little doubt that the Falasha Jews of Ethiopia were also originally converted by Jewish missionaries, over a thousand years ago.

This missionary zeal, however, evaporated after the destruction of the Jewish State in the year 70. For the most part, during the past thousand years, Jews have been more intent on preserving their heritage than on adding to their numbers through conversion. Often, in fact, potential candidates for conversion were discouraged by the rabbis who warned that the demands of the Jewish religion were great and the burden of being a Jew in an intolerant world was not easy to bear. Nevertheless, throughout our history some conversions to Judaism have continued to take place and they are not altogether uncommon today.

Our tradition makes no distinction between Jews born into Judaism and those who were accepted into our faith. Several of the ancient rabbis, in fact, including some of those who created the *Talmud*, traced their ancestry to Gentiles who had been converted to Judaism.

Why Does Judaism Oppose Intermarriage?

RELIGIOUS Jews oppose intermarriage for the same reasons that motivate the devout of all faiths. Differences of religion between husband and wife present a serious obstacle to a truly harmonious relationship; such marriages, even when they endure, impose a constant strain on the religious loyalties of both partners, and raise serious personal and family problems difficult to solve.

A happy marriage must be based on a unity of spirit. When husband and wife disagree on an issue as crucial as their religious creed, the chances for a durable, satisfying relationship are very poor. And the children of such a marriage are subjected to the grave conflict of having to choose between the deepest convictions of the two people dearer to them than anyone else in the world.

An eminent Reform rabbi of the nineteenth century expressed it this way: "Little as any true friend of religion and humanity could wish that religion should stand between those who sincerely love and cling to each other . . . still from the standpoint of religion and of a sincere religious life, he cannot but disapprove of mixed marriages."

Quite aside from the important personal consideration of harmony in marriage, Jews are opposed to intermarriage because of its threat to the future of Judaism. A minority faith finds it more necessary than those with greater numbers to preserve its identity by resisting the inroads of intermarriage.

What Is the Jewish Attitude Towards Christmas?

As A religious celebration in commemoration of the birth of Jesus, Christmas has no significance whatsoever for Jews, since the most basic point of difference between Judaism and Christianity lies in the Christian belief in the divinity of Jesus.

In our modern world, however, Christmas has taken on increasingly secular overtones which tend to envelop all of society.

The elaborate exchange of Christmas gifts, so vehemently and persistently encouraged by commercial interests; the preponderance of beautifully decorated Christmas trees in public places; and the widespread introduction of Christmas plays, songs, carols, window displays, greeting cards and other manifestations of the season, make it impossible for anyone who leaves the confines of his own home or tunes in on a radio or television set during the month of December not to share in some aspects of the Christmas celebration.

Indeed, the spirit of friendship and good fellowship that abounds at Christmas is one in which all men of good will can happily join.

But sensitive Jews and Christians alike deplore the growing secularization of the Christmas holiday, since it tends to obliterate, *for both*, the important *religious* connotations of the occasion. In the spiritual observance of Christmas, Jews cannot share—any more than non-Jews can share in the observance of Rosh Hashanah or Yom Kippur.

Are Synagogue Services Open Only to Jews?

THERE is a rather common notion among non-Jews that the synagogue is a place of mystery—exclusive and inaccessible to all but the faithful. Actually this belief is completely unwar-

ranted. Any one may enter a synagogue and at any time. Inscribed over the altars of many Jewish houses of worship are
the words of Isaiah: "My House shall be a House for all
peoples."

In an Orthodox or Conservative synagogue where worshipers pray with heads covered, a non-Jewish visitor may wish to
keep his hat on too, for the sake of conformity. But even this
is not required.

Non-Jews who attend the service may also join in the
prayers—if they wish. Most Christians will find a good deal
that is familiar in the synagogue ritual. A Conservative congregation recites the 145th Psalm: "The Lord is nigh unto all that
call upon Him, to all that call upon Him in truth. . . ." In a Reform Temple, the congregants repeat another prayer universal
in appeal: "Grant peace, Thy most precious gift, O Thou
eternal source of peace . . ."

Even the distinctly Jewish prayers such as the mourner's
Kaddish strike a responsive chord in men of all faiths: "May
the Father of peace send peace to all who mourn, and comfort
the bereaved among us."

During the past decade, Christian youth groups of every denomination have visited synagogues and temples in their own
communities. Invariably they have found the rabbis happy to
explain the various symbols in the sanctuary and to contribute
to their appreciation and understanding of Judaism as the well-
spring of Christianity.

No one, whatever his faith, need hesitate about entering a
synagogue or temple, to observe, to study, to meditate—or, if
he so wishes, to pray.

Are Jews Permitted to Attend Church Services or Pray with Persons of Other Faiths?

MANY Jews have attended church with Christian friends and neighbors, both for the regular Sunday or holiday services and for the special ceremonies attendant on weddings, confirmations, funerals and the like. They go to church, however, as visitors, not as participants. Observant Jews do not join in the services; and under no circumstances will they kneel during the services, even for the sake of conformity, because the position of genuflection is sternly forbidden in Jewish worship. (The only exception to this rule is for the Cantor who recites the Adoration prayer on the Day of Atonement.) Jewish children are taught that in ancient times some of their forefathers chose martyrdom when under force to kneel at prayer.

Most Jews, on the other hand, will participate in interfaith or community religious services, so long as the prayers, Bible readings and hymns are acceptable to both Christian and Jew.

On numerous occasions churches have been used for Jewish religious services. Often in the free atmosphere of the United States, a church or synagogue will offer its hospitality to a neighboring congregation of another faith, especially when that group is in the process of building its own house of worship, or has had it damaged by fire or other calamity. Military chapels are also used interchangeably by Christians and Jews, taking care to remove all sectarian symbols during the hour of worship.

Judaism, generally, does not approve of excessive praying. An ancient rabbi was once asked why one should not pray every hour, since worship was good for the soul. He answered with a parable about a monarch whose subjects praised him with monotonous regularity and frequency. The King of Kings, declared the rabbi, did not wish His name extolled at every moment out of sheer habit, rather than true reverence.

How Does a Non-Jew Become a Jew?

As a rabbi, I have often had occasion to participate in the conversion of non-Jews, both Catholic and Protestant, to Judaism. Most frequently, the motivating factor is an interreligious marriage and the desire of the non-Jewish partner to share the faith of the loved one. Not infrequently, however, rabbis are approached by non-Jewish men and women who, through their own studies and experiences, have decided that Judaism offers to them the best medium of religious expression.

Contrary to popular misconception, the steps to conversion are far from formidable. In the Orthodox ritual the convert appears before a rabbi, in the presence of two other learned men or rabbis, and makes the following declaration: (1) that he knows and accepts the duties and obligations of Jewish law and sincerely intends to fulfill them; (2) that he rejects those tenets of his former faith that are out of keeping with Judaism;

(3) that he has been baptized in the traditional ritual bath; and (4) that he has been circumcised.

The Reform ritual is also not elaborate. The candidate for conversion is required to answer seven questions: (1) that he enters Judaism of his own free will; (2) that he is willing to renounce his former faith; (3) that he will pledge his loyalty to Judaism; (4) that he promises "to cast his lot with the people of Israel amid all circumstances and conditions"; (5) that he will lead a Jewish life; (6) that he will rear his children in the Jewish faith; and (7) that he will have his male children circumcised. The candidate then makes a formal pledge and repeats, in English and in Hebrew, the prayer: "Hear O Israel, the Lord our God, the Lord is One."

Before he can be accepted into Judaism the candidate must prove that he is familiar with the faith which he has chosen. He must have completed an intensive course of studies, including the Bible, the prayer book, customs and rituals, holiday and Sabbath observances, and Jewish history. The modern convert to Judaism often knows more about his faith than one who is born a Jew and takes his religion for granted.

The Orthodox ritual calls for the new initiate to attend the synagogue on the Sabbath following his conversion. He is called to the reading of the *Torah*, and a special blessing is recited: "May he who blessed our ancestor, Abraham, *the first convert*, and said to him: 'Go thou before Me and be righteous,' bless and give courage to this convert who enters the fold." He is then given a Hebrew name for use in all ritual acts.

This ceremony is the last reference ever made to the man's conversion. It is forbidden by Jewish law to remind him of his former status, or to speak disrespectfully of it.

[IX]

TODAY AND TOMORROW

Oh, Lord,
I wish I loved the greatest saint
As much as You, God,
Love the greatest sinner.
            Rabbi Shlomo Karliner

Are There Hasidim Today?

A FAIR ESTIMATE of the total number of Hasidim in the world would be close to a quarter of a million. Their largest concentration is in the United States and in Israel, but they are well represented in England, France, Australia and Morocco.

Although there are at least a score of Hasidic groups, the major ones are the Lubavitcher, the Satmar, the Bobover and the Gerer. In each case, the name of their spiritual leader— hence their group name—is derived from that of their ancestral home in Eastern Europe. Disciples of each Rebbe (the leader is called "Rebbe" rather than "Rabbi" as it represents a more intimate Yiddish title) tend to cluster in neighborhoods: the Lubavitcher in the Crown Heights section of Brooklyn; an entire housing development in Rechovot, Israel, contains several thousand followers of the Gerer Rebbe; a town near the west bank of the Hudson River in New York State bears the name "Square Town," an anglicization of Skver, the Polish city from which their Rebbe emigrated.

A simplistic definition of Hasidism might well be "Judaism with soul." Hasidim believe that the human soul is a gift of God, a temporary gift which enables human beings to share in the divine essence. Man's finite mind prevents him from understanding the full nature of the mystery. Through study and prayer, the Jews, whose relationship with God is in itself a special divine gift, can catch a glimpse of that truth. The soul is both emotion and intellect. The true Hasid loses himself in rapture (the English word "enthusiasm" literally mean "losing oneself in God") in the sheer joy of practicing the *mitzvahs* (divine commands) and in the study of God's Law.

In 1969, a newspaper reporter estimated that there were approximately 150,000 followers the Lubavitcher Rebbe. Unquestionably, they are the most influential and the best known of the Hasidic groups. Their spiritual leader is Rabbi Menachem Schneersohn, a direct descendant of one of the eighteenth-century original founders of the Hasidic movement. Rabbi Schneersohn was born in 1902, and, oddly enough, received an advanced degree from the Sorbonne University in Paris, despite the fact that his followers are not encouraged to engage in college studies. His disciples refer to him simply as *the* Rebbe, it being clearly understood that they are referring to the Saint of Eastern Parkway in Brooklyn. When prime ministers and presidents of Israel visit America, they invariably make a pilgrimage to his home.

The most elaborate and detailed philosophy of the Hasidim is to be found in the publications of the Lubavitcher group. Hasidim use Yiddish, rather than Hebrew or a secular language, as their language of communication. Only the Lubavitcher group publishes extensively in English, French and other languages. The Rebbe trains hundreds, perhaps thousands, of disciples who carry word of the Hasidim to the far corners of the earth. A distinctive feature of the Lubavitcher is their *outreach*. Unlike other Hasidim, who tend to remain in isolation even from other Jews, the followers of the Rebbe have no fear of being corrupted by contact with unbelieving or completely secular Jews. On the contrary, the maintain an ambitious and energetic program of bringing the message to those who have strayed from their traditional faith.

The approach of Lubavitcher teachers is based on patience and tolerance. They neither reproach nor condemn the "unfaithful," but seek to bring them to the truth, step by step, urging them to observe one *mitzvah*, one commandment, at a time: a single act of dietary observance, the donning of phylacteries by men, the kindling of Sabbath candles by the women. By extensive use of "religious mobile homes," the teachers reach out to hundreds of college campuses and areas of Jewish concentration to distribute small gifts for the Feast of Purim, unleavened bread on Passover and a variety of ritual objects that often represent the very first contact which some young Jews have with ceremonial rites.

Their American outreach has brought them to twenty-nine states. Young rabbis are dispatched by the Rebbe to a community (I use the word "dispatch" advisedly, because a number of them, having spent all of their lives in a tiny area of Brooklyn, have only a vague idea of such exotic places as Memphis, Tennessee, or Phoenix, Arizona) to set up centers for study and worship. Financed initially by their international office, the young teachers raise funds and establish *Chabad* Houses. The key word in the movement, *Chabad*, is an acronym for three words meaning Wisdom, Understanding and Knowledge. The Hasid (disciple) explains that these three words are but partial reflections of the true essence of their beliefs. The soul is both emotion and belief. "Soul-power," a phrase used by the Rebbe, involves both "delight" and "will"— the thrill which comes from a realization that we are sparks of the Divine, and the will which comes from use of our God-given intellect. (Incidentally, a Hasid spells the divine name, G–d, in deference to the commandment about using the Lord's name in vain.)

Although the second largest group, the followers of the Satmar Rebbe, oppose the establishment of the State of Israel because it might delay the advent of the Messiah, the Lubavitcher group support Israel, and many of them believe that the rebirth of the Jewish state and the return to the Holy Land represent the "footsteps of the Messiah," the early beginnings of the Messianic Age.

When will the Messiah come? At any time—perhaps tomorrow. He will be of "flesh and blood." He will rebuild the Temple of Solomon on Zion's Heights and will gather all the children of Israel from "the four corners of the earth."

Some critics of the Hasidic movement object to its so-called personality cult, its blind obedience to the Rebbe. From the lips of young rabbis who have been sent to virtually every major community in America, one hears of their total and unquestioning acceptance of the Lubavitcher Rebbe's authority. His gifts as a seer enable him to send a message to a disciple, summoning him to travel to a remote community, where, invariably, he will find a single Jewish soul in need of spiritual guidance. These disciples are committed to the age-old tradition that "he who saves a single soul is as if he had redeemed all of mankind."

A disciple of the Rebbe does not begin a major undertaking in his personal life without seeking guidance from the Rebbe. Through direct contact or, more often, through mail or telephone, he will seek the Rebbe's opinion before surgery, prior to choosing a marriage partner or before a major business or professional action. The Rebbe's powers of "seeing from afar" are based on his total submergence in the *Torah*, in studying the word of God. Each letter of the sacred writings is a window to the will of God. Therefore, one year, when the Rebbe informed thirty-six families that he expected them to move to Israel, they accepted the mandate without hesitation.

Despite the wide scope of its international outreach, all activities of this Hasidim are low-key. An academy of higher learning was established in Casablanca, Morocco, without fanfare or publicity. Following the Castro revolution in Cuba, quiet contact was made with the remnant of Jews in Havana. Similarly, the Hasidic strategy, with regard to Soviet and Russian-satellite Jewry, is to make contact in an undramatic fashion. The Rebbe is convinced that open demonstrations against Communist treatment of Jews is counterproductive. Somehow, contact is arranged with individual Jews (the ways of the Rebbe are a mystery) and, as the disciples emerge into lands of freedom, they are helped both spiritually and materially. Through their organization called FREE (Friends of Refugees from Eastern Europe), educational programs are conducted to teach Hebrew and the principles of the faith, the uncircumcised men are circumcised, summer camps are established for the young, furniture is provided for the destitute, and jobs are found in their new homes.

When I asked one of his rabbi-disciples how the Rebbe had received his gifts of intercession through prayer, he explained that his master was a *Zaddik,* an utterly righteous human being who possessed all the qualities of the patriarch Abraham, and of Moses. Abraham, the founder of the faith, went one step beyond his progenitor, Noah. Noah, when faced with the sinful generation of the Flood, contented himself with building an ark for himself and his family. Abraham, on the other hand, interceded with the Almighty on behalf of the sinners of Sodom. Moses went the final step: he pleaded for all his peo-

ple: "Blot me out but save my people." The mutual bond between Abraham, Moses and the Rebbe is that they *care* for
humanity!

How Many Jews Are There in the World?

THERE IS probably no way to count the number of Jews
in any given area, let alone the total Jewish population in the
world. Every demographic study, a considerable number of
which have appeared in recent years, refers to newly refined
methods of determining the Jewish population in the community. In each of these studies, the word "estimated" is
added, because of the many pitfalls that stand in the way of a
scientific survey.

For example, whenever American Census Bureau statisticians
sought to include a question on religious preference in their
decennial polls, official Jewish bodies have vigorously opposed
it. To my mind, these implicit fears that government identification of Jews might possibly lead to the kind of discrimination
experienced in other parts of the world are a manifestation of
overreaction. It seems to me that it would be useful to obtain
accurate information about the number of Jews in America.

A major question harks back to the very first one raised in
this book: What is a Jew? In the 1974–1975 American Jewish
Year Book, Dr. Fred Massarik, America's foremost Jewish
demographer, reported that the National Jewish Population
Study of 1970 *estimated* that the Jewish population of the

United States stood at 5,800,000. That figure was based on the number of Jewish households. Then, Dr. Massarik added: "If the estimate is adjusted to exclude non-Jewish persons residing in Jewish households, such as non-Jewish spouses and children who are not being raised as Jews, the total number is . . . 5,370,000."

On the other hand, a leading actuary, who is vice-president of one of the nation's largest insurance companies, told me that he believed that there were about ten million Americans of Jewish parentage!

The exclusive use of the religious definition to determine the Jewish population is a far from infallible method. Less than half of the American Jews are formally affiliated with a congregation. In former days, one of the tests was referred to as the "Yom Kippur test," since most nonaffiliated Jews observed the holiest days in the religious calendar. This is no longer a reliable technique.

During the time I served as head of the Jewish Military Association, we made representations to the Defense Department in the matter of determining the number of Jewish chaplains required by the armed services. The Pentagon agreed with our view that even those Jews without religious affiliation would seek out a rabbi to officiate at weddings and funerals, or for counseling in family matters.

In the forty community studies (covering over 95 percent of the nation's Jewish population) that have been published during the past twenty-five years, the basic criterion for identification has been neither religious nor ethnic, but the *practical* one proposed in my answer to the first question in this book. The demographers generally include all those who consider themselves Jews.

Recent statistics indicate that there are 5,845,000 Jews in the

United States. The world Jewish population totals 14,144,000. Within the United States, two discernible shifts are apparent: a vast movement from the inner cities to the suburbs as well as a steady stream to warmer climates. California contains far more Jews—662,000—than any *country* other than the United States in the free world! It is not an exaggeration to say that the climate in which contemporary Jews live is from ten to twenty degrees warmer than that of their grandparents. In 1900, most of world Jewry lived in the snow-packed regions of Russia and Poland. Three million of their grandchildren have settled in the semitropical clime of Israel, and well over one million Jews have made their homes in balmy parts of the United States from Florida to California.

Why Do Jews Persist in Keeping Alive Memories of the Holocaust?

MUCH CRITICISM has been directed against contemporary Jews who seem to have a morbid preoccupation with memories of the Holocaust, the annihilation of six million Jews during World War II. Granted, the destruction of almost 40 percent of the world Jewish population, within the period of less than a decade, was a lacerating experience for those who survived. Hundreds of books have been written which reflect the emotional scars of wives and husbands, parents and children of those who were lost in the Nazi death chambers. For millions of Jews, the manner of the death of their loved ones evokes feelings that time does not heal.

But the question still persists: Is there anything productive in *institutionalizing* the Holocaust by setting aside a special Holocaust Day each spring; in establishing courses in high schools, universities, synagogues and centers devoted to Holocaust studies; in creating a worldwide organization with headquarters in Vienna to track down the operators of death camps who escaped punishment? Even the liturgy of the synagogue has been transformed by the Holocaust. In the newest prayer book published by Reform Judaism, special passages have been added for observance of *Yom Hashoah*, Holocaust Day, which call upon worshipers to affirm that "the world is not the same since Auschwitz." Is not such protracted concentration on past persecution a form of morbidity?

There are three reasons why Jews have perpetuated memories of the Holocaust: historical, practical and moral.

I observed in earlier chapters that Jews are a history-oriented people. Anniversaries have always figured prominently in the consciousness of the Jew. His personal calendar included not only birthdays and wedding anniversaries but also anniversaries of the death of dear ones. In my youth, I joined with my parents in attending community observances of the anniversaries of the death of Theodore Herzl, founder of modern Zionism, and of Chaim Bialik, poet laureate of the Jewish people. In the twelfth century, the philosopher Maimonides set aside an annual reminder of the day when his ship was saved on its perilous journey from Morocco to Palestine. "The past," wrote Irsael Zangwill, "is our cradle, not our prison. The past is for inspiration, not imitation."

Undoubtedly, we can assume that in future centuries, Jews will gather in synagogues and communal centers on the twenty-seventh day of the Hebrew month of Nisan (which occurs either in April or May) to commemorate the twentieth-century Holocaust, to carry on this tradition just as the fast on the Day of the destruction of the Temple at Jerusalem has continued for the past nineteen-hundred years.

Beyond the historical reason for memorializing the Holocaust is the practical one. A Protestant theologian suggested that "the Jews will begin to forget when we Christians begin to remember." If, as the philosopher George Santayana remarked, those who ignore history are condemned to repeat the mistakes of history, it is incumbent on those who would build a decent world to contemplate the tragedy of the Nazi era in order to avoid a repetition of the disaster.

The horrors of the Nazi concentration camps are so mind-shattering that we find it overwhelming to fix attention upon them for any extended period of time. The psychological temptation is so powerful to create the fantasy that the events never actually took place that some academicians have written books which negate the evidence of tens of thousands of eye-witnesses as well as of official Nazi documents confirming the systematic annihilation of six million Jews.

Through the dedicated efforts of a Simon Wiesenthal in gathering this evidence, and by the building of memorials in Paris and in Jerusalem, mankind is offered the opportunity to set straight the historical record.

But, overarching it all, the moral reason is the most important one. When the mass-murderer, Karl Adolf Eichmann, was on trial, the Israelis informed the world that the motive of the judicial proceedings was not vengeance, but the moral education of contemporary man. Civilized men in the postwar era came to the realization, as they contemplated the events of 1936–1945, that the sin of omission on the part of the decent peoples of the world was the sin of silence, the refusal to believe that a highly enlightened people like the Germans could permit themselves to be led by a madman into acts of national depravity which culminated in the events of Auschwitz and Buchenwald.

I shall never forget the words of a leading official of the National Council of Churches during an address to an audience of Protestant editors of Sunday School textbooks: "Sometimes, when I can't sleep, I agonize over the question: The men who turned on the gas in the Nazi gas chambers—where were they, on a Sunday morning, when they were eleven years old? Were they in church, and what did they learn about Jews that would enable them, without a trace of remorse, to turn the gas on innocent children?"

The moral reason for preserving memories of the Holocaust beyond our lifetime was best expressed by David Ben-Gurion: "We ask the nations of the world not to forget that one million babies, because they happened to be Jews, were murdered. We want the nations of the world to know that there was an intention to exterminate a people. That intention had its roots in anti-Semitism. They should know that anti-Semitism is dangerous and they should be ashamed of it."

For Jews—and for mankind, too—to recall the death of six million victims is not to brood in bitterness or to dwell on man's capacity for inhumanity, but to seek to draw lessons from the past that will enable humanity to build the new order envisioned by Isaiah "in which none shall be afraid."

What Accounts for the Agitation of World Jewry on Behalf of Soviet Jews?

ONE FIFTH of the Jewish population of the world lives under the domination of Communist rule. A generation ago, three million Jews lived in Poland. Today, in that Soviet-dominated country, their number, largely as a result of Hitler's extermination policy, has been reduced to nine thousand. Those Polish Jews who survived the death chambers felt no inclination to return to totalitarian rule. Jews see in the suppression of freedom for millions of their co-religionists in the Soviet Union a continuation of the Holocaust, not in terms of physical destruction but of spiritual and intellectual dissolution of a Jewish community that for centuries was the leading source of Jewish cultural creativity and religious observance.

When I visited Russia in 1956, I found hardly a trace of that historic tradition. The Communist regime had systematically destroyed organized Jewish life. All opportunities had been eliminated for religious nurture of the young. The publication of Jewish religious and cultural materials had been suppressed. A mood of fear had been created among those who wished to practice their faith.

Since the death of Stalin, restrictions against religious observance have been somewhat eased, but Judaism continues to be a target of governmental suppression. The Greek Orthodox Church is permitted to function, even though attendance at worship remains meager. State subsidies provide for the maintenance of seminaries to train priests and for the publication of prayer books, Bibles and textbooks.

Russia's main objection to the faith and traditions of the Jews is that they are not locally oriented. Like the Roman Catholics, their spiritual ties and loyalties lie beyond the tightly closed borders of the Communist world. The Soviet Union was among the first nations to recognize the newborn State of Israel. But Kremlin leaders soon realized that Israel evoked a kind of attachment on the part of Russian Jews which ran counter to Communist ideology. The persistent demand made by many Jews to leave the "Marxist paradise" kindled the same kind of resistance which led its satellite, East Germany, to erect a Berlin Wall between the East and the West. And when, within the space of a decade, 150,000 Jews chose to emigrate, Communist leaders recognized in their departure a genuine threat to their long-cherished principles.

Jewish communities in the Free World are exerting strenuous efforts on behalf of their fellow Jews in the Soviet Union, and endeavoring to persuade the Russian government to offer basic human rights to its citizens and to grant them the privilege of emigration.

In the United States, two organizations have been formed to develop public awareness of the plight of Russian Jews. The National Conference of Soviet Jewry has been particularly active in forming local community programs throughout the country. On a very large scale, Jews in Denver, Boston, Dallas, and a score of other cities maintain regular correspondence with individual Soviet Jewish citizens. Jewish tourists visiting Moscow, Leningrad, Kiev and Odessa, where most of their coreligionists live, are encouraged to visit their homes. Leaders of the movement in the United States are convinced that agitation on behalf of their brethren will make the Kremlin aware that their actions are subject to the scrutiny of enlightened people everywhere.

A second organization, the Union of Communities on Soviet Jewry, based in Washington, maintains a political lobby to enlist the support of legislators. Some senators and congressmen have sponsored individual immigration applications of Russian Jews. American Jews, under the guidance of the organization, have placed overseas phone calls (not too easy a task) to "refuseniks"—those who have been penalized for their temerity in applying for exit visas by loss of jobs and incarceration. The Russian government, sensitive to public opinion, has frequently yielded to such exposure of their actions by granting to a considerable number of persons the right to emigrate.

Those who have agitated on behalf of Soviet Jewry believe that their most important objective is to convey to their fellow Jews behind the Iron Curtain the feeling that they are not completely isolated, and that many Jews in the Free World are engaged in a concerted attempt to liberate them from their shackles. In Jewish tradition, one basic *mitzvah* (divine command) is called *pidyon shvuyim*, the ransoming of captives. Throughout the Middle Ages, every congregation set aside funds, collected on the eve of Sabbath, for the purpose of fulfilling the *mitzvah*. That tradition continues in the worldwide struggle for Free World Jewry on behalf of their coreligionists in Russia.

Is There a Jewish Position
on Conscientious Objection to War?

I PREFACE my answer to these questions with a note of apology. I am both mortified and mystified by the absence of this question in all previous editions of this book. Mortified, because it seems incredible that a book on Jewish beliefs would contain no reference to the Jewish concept of peace. To write about Judaism without using the word, *sholom*, is tantamount to presenting a study of the American principles without mentioning the Declaration of Independence. I am mystified because, after thirty-eight printings of the book involving a half-million copies, not a single reader pointed out the deficiency. Recently, one of my students at Mesa [Arizona] Community College, an airman at Williams Air Force Base who is not of the Jewish faith, drew my attention to this obvious oversight.

Like Christianity, Judaism is subject to a wide range of interpretations as to what is the authentic faith. Some Jews translate the basic doctrine of *sholom* (peace) into a rejection of any resort to violence against human beings. Hence, during World War II, American synagogue groups endorsed the position of a number of young Jews drafted into military service who indicated a record of religious conviction as it applied to

227

the principle of nonviolence.

The sanctity of human life has been a historic element in Jewish teaching. (Refer to the chapter on capital punishment, page 37.) But Judaism, since ancient times, has distinguished between "obligatory military action" and "permissive war." Though the Talmud speaks of "be killed rather than kill," the reference is to a situation in which a sword is placed against a man's back, and another in his hand, with the order to murder another human being. But Talmudic law declares that self-defense is a perfectly moral ground for killing.

Hence, Jewish tradition would support the bearing of arms when a nation is at war. An ethical problem arises when two basic principles are in conflict. Jewish religious law affirms that "the law of the land is Jewish law." What if one's nation is engaged in an immoral war? What is the obligation, for instance, of a Jewish citizen under Nazi rule? The *Talmud* supplies an answer to the dilemma by distinguishing between "a wicked government" and a "righteous government." In the case of the former, one must obey one's conscience rather than the state.

During the Vietnam War, the question arose among both church and synagogue members as to whether there could be "selective conscientious objection," which entailed a subjective evaluation of the morality of a specific government action. The problem was not fully resolved.

At all events, Judaism does allow for conscientious objection to war. And it finds warrant in the Bible (Deut. 20), which lists exemptions for those who are too weak for military duty, interpreting "weakness" to include those who have no stomach for bloodshed.

Perhaps the most eloquent testimony to the idea of *sholom* is reflected in the oft-repeated words of the former Prime

Minister of Israel, Golda Meir: "I can find it in my heart to forgive the Arabs for killing our sons, but I can never forgive them for making killers out of our sons."

What Is a Mitzvah?

IF ONE WERE to look for a single word to catch the spirit of Judaism it would be summarized in the idea of *mitzvah*. Technically, it means "a divine command." Or, as the prophet Micah expressed it: "What does the Lord require of you?"

The Jewish faith has little room for such experiences as finding God in a momentary flash of discovery. The essence of Judaism is a day-to-day, hour-by-hour practicing of *mitzvos* (plural of *mitzvah*)—good deeds that are pleasing in the sight of God. Authentic religious experience for the Jew is the joyous feeling: "I performed a *mitzvah*"—an act of kindness, of compassion, of justice, of consideration for another human being!"

Of course, many a *mitzvah* is a ritualistic act: the eating of unleavened bread on Passover, or dwelling in a *succah* during the Feast of Tabernacles, or kindling the Sabbath candles. Yet each of these acts is a means to a moral end. The Passover rites are the symbolic clothing for the ideal of freedom; the building of a temporary hut for the Festival of Tabernacles is a symbolic reminder of the temporary nature of human existence as well as a call to thanksgiving for God's bounty. Rituals such as kindling the Sabbath candles reflect the ideal of family unity.

For some Jews, the mechanical observance of all God's commands may seem sufficient. But, since the days of the ancient prophets, the heart of the Jewish faith lies in the *mitzvah* performed in our relations with fellow men. In answer to the prophetic question, "What does the Lord require of you?" Micah answered, "Only to do justice, to love mercy and to walk humbly." And eighteen-hundred years ago, the rabbis stressed that a *mitzvah* must not be performed out of a sense of duty, but for its own sake. "Don't be like servants who act in order to receive a reward from their masters, but like those who expect nothing in return."

In summary, the truly religious Jew is one who has cultivated the gift of finding fulfillment in following God's design for living. "Who is pleasing in God's sight? He who is pleasing in the sight of Man." The Psalmist sang: "The precepts of the Lord are right, rejoicing the heart."

In a joyous acceptance of the burden of *mitzvahs*, the sincere Jew lives up to the demands of his faith. The ideal life for him is a string of *mitzvahs* performed every day. There are no twice-born Jews.

Why Are There Different Ways of Spelling the Jewish Holidays?

THE SCIENCE of linguistics has taught us a great deal about the different sound values given to the same letters of the alphabet by various languages. George Bernard Shaw's character, Professor Higgins, reminded us, too, of the infinite varieties among the dialects of the same language.

When I am asked the correct spelling of a Jewish holiday, I

generally reply that there is no "correct" one, only a spectrum of different spellings. Professor Werner Weinberg's book *How Do You Spell Chanukah?* is a scholarly attempt to introduce a standardization of spelling—what he calls "the Romanization of Hebrew letters." I once calculated that there are 1,050 different ways to spell "Chanukah," not counting a few French variants.

A further complication is added by the differences between pronunciation in Hebrew of Ashkenazic (Eastern Central European) Jews and Sephardic (Mediterranean and Oriental) Jews. The present trend among Jews throughout the world is to follow the latter pronunciation, since it has been adopted in Israel.

The correct spelling, that is, transliteration or transcription, of a Hebrew word or name would be one which the reader recognizes by the sound he senses when his eyes fall upon the word. To the English-speaking Jew, *Yom Kippur* is an accurate phonetic reflection of the Hebrew words for the Day of Atonement. The French reader finds Yom *Kippour* closest to the phonetic value he gives to the Hebrew words.

Over the centuries, some Hebrew sounds have entirely evaporated. The now silent letter, *ayin,* was pronounced in biblical days. To the Greeks, it had a guttural sound to which they assigned the letter *g.* So the city of 'Aza became Gaza, and the sinful town of 'Amorrah was rendered Gomorrah.

In any event, there is no uniform spelling of "Chanukah." When I am asked for the absolutely correct spelling, I occasionally respond: "The most accurate one is *chet, nun, kaf, heh.*"

Has the Women's Liberation Movement Affected the Religious Status of the Jewish Woman?

PROFESSOR BLU GREENBERG, a leader in the Jewish woman's liberation movement, has written that "the Jewish woman is now four thousand years old; whether she has yet come of age is still a matter of solemn debate."

In the past quarter century, some very concrete progress has been visible in equalizing the status of the Jewish woman in the eyes of Jewish tradition and customs. A score of Reform temples and a few Conservative ones have elected women as presidents and senior officers on their boards. In 1972, the Hebrew Union College (Reform) ordained a woman as a rabbi; several others have been ordained since. It is estimated that 30 percent of the students currently enrolled in liberal seminaries are female.

Within the Conservative movement, a great deal of agitation has produced considerable change. Classic Jewish law virtually excluded women from a role in synagogue affairs. They were not obligated to participate in communal worship, and were, therefore, ineligible to participate in the Reading of the *Torah*. Recently, the Rabbinical Assembly has modified its stand on calling women to the altar for the Reading of the *Torah* ritual. However, by leaving the decision for change to the discretion of the individual congregation, the rabbinic group opened the door only minimally to feminine involvement, and there has been more controversy than progress.

In the realm of marriage and divorce laws, adhered to by both Orthodox and Conservative Jewry, the inequality of such rights as the initiation of divorce proceedings has been acutely felt in recent years. The Conservative rabbinate has altered the law of abandonment, which forbade a Jewish wife to remarry when her husband had disappeared.

In 1973, the first National Conference of Jewish Women was launched, and its journal, *Response*, published. The following year, the Jewish Feminist Organization was created as a national movement, with the stated goal of: "the full, direct and equal participation of women at all levels of Jewish life—communal, religious, educational and political."

One can appreciate the depth of resentment on the part of modern Jewish women, when, as late as 1970, in a book published in England, Rabbi Immanuel Jakobovitz wrote that "the wife is required by Jewish religious law to 'give the income of her work' and all of her inheritance to her husband, while the husband is only under the obligation to support her throughout her life." The Chief Rabbi of the British Commonwealth quoted this rabbinic law without passing judgment on its equity.

Inevitably, a ferment for change has developed within Orthodox Jewish circles. As a result of the entrance of more Orthodox women into the world of higher education and into many professions, dissatisfaction with the status quo has become evident. If men exclude women from the realm of public prayer and relegate them to synagogue seats behind curtained barriers, why not, as some have suggested, establish all-female congregations?

Professor Saul Berman, Head of the Department of Judaic Studies at an Orthodox-sponsored college, reports that "a small number of religious women have begun donning *tallith* [prayer shawls] and *terfillin* [phylacteries] daily." Dr. Berman insists that "it is vital for religious leadership to recognize the reality of the religious quest of Jewish women . . . . Women must be made to feel that their own religious development is a vital concern of communal leadership."

Dr. Blu Greenberg (quoted above) is the wife of an eminent Orthodox rabbi who recognizes that change within traditional Judaism can only be effected through revisions in *Halachah* (religious law) by competent authorities. She writes that contemporary Jewish women, with ready access to classic legal sources, can themselves undertake the role of religious authorities. "Women *poskim* [religious decision-makers] are more likely than men to find sympathetic solutions to women's problems. . . . Considering how far the *Halachah* will begin to grow and stretch to meet women's needs and overcome disabilities, women *poskim* are essential. And the notion of women rabbis must be accepted in all branches of Judaism."

The more traditional Conservative bodies are now actively pondering the possible ordination of women as rabbis. We can assume that, by century's end, the age-old relegation of Jewish women to second-class religious status will have disappeared.

Why Is Jerusalem So Important to the Jewish People?

JERUSALEM is in the unfortunate position of a mother with two daughters, both of whom lay moral claim to their maternal home. For the past three thousand years, Jews have lived in the City of David, hallowing it, not so much as the national capital of their homeland, but as the spiritual center of their faith. In mystic tradition, Jerusalem was the very center of the universe, the gathering place of the faithful "at the end of day," when messianic redemption comes for all mankind.

Three times a day, 365 days a year, Jews prayed for the well-being of Jerusalem. Grooms and brides exchanged vows with the blessing that joy would return to the Holy City. Mourners at a graveside would be comforted with the prayer that they would share in the consolation of those "who mourn for Jerusalem." From time immemorial, the pious would arrange for burial in the "consecrated earth of the Holy City." And, on the most festive occasion of the year, Passover, Jews would leave the *Seder* table with the chant: "Next year in Jerusalem!"

Modern man finds it difficult to grasp the validity of a tradition that has endured thousands of years. In an age when a single generation produces revolutionary changes, one finds it almost incomprehensible that the Jewish people should retain in the forefront of their consciousness patriarchs who lived four thousand years ago and should nurture their children to regard ancient prophets and sages as daily companions. Part of the very furniture of their lives were the words and thoughts of men and women who lived hundreds of years ago. Thus, the concept, "temporary," has an altogether different meaning for Jews than it does in today's thought-world. When, in the year 70 C.E., the Romans drove the Jews of Palestine into exile, the very word "exile" (*galut*), became an integral part of the vocabulary, and entered immediately into the liturgy of the synagogue.

There were times when Jerusalem held no Jewish inhabitants. In 1099, Arab invaders massacred every Jewish (and Christian) resident of the Holy City. In succeeding centuries, Jews never abandoned their moral rights to Jerusalem. The claim of the invaders that the city was holy to the worshipers of Allah had a hollow ring. Moslem pretensions to the City of David were *derivative*. Mohammed, the founder of Islam, beckoned the faithful to turn toward Jerusalem in prayer only because he had read the *Jewish* Holy Book. The spiritual right of Moslems to Jerusalem was based on a vision of their Prophet that he had flown through the air from Arabia and had descended on the spot where the Mosque of Omar stands. Fantasy had taken him—not to Rome or Athens—but to the place of Solomon's Temple, held sacred by the ancient faith of Israel!

In contrast, the other daughter religion, Christianity, has substantial emotional roots in the city. Gethsemane and Golgotha were the very cradles of their faith.

Aside from historical and religious attachments to Jerusalem, there are considerable legal and political grounds for the Jewish claim to the Holy City. Except for brief times, as mentioned above, when they were forbidden access to Jerusalem, Jews have lived in the ancient capital continuously. Few people realize that the majority of the population has been Jewish since 1844. In 1948, the year of Israel's birth, Jews outnumbered Moslems by 100,000 to 40,000. As early as 1922, there were approximately three times as many Jews than Moslems in the city. Politically, Arabs never regarded Jerusalem as their capital; Ramle was the center of their administration.

When Transjordan's King Abdullah laid siege to Jerusalem in 1948, the Jewish defenders fought with a ferocity that cost many lives, for they sensed that Arab domination of the Old City would deny them access to their holy shrines—the Western Wall, the Tower of David, the Tombs of Rachel and of the Patriarchs. From 1948 to 1967, their worst fears were realized. Jewish gravestones on the Mount of Olives were used as highway building blocks, scores of synagogues where Jews had prayed for many centuries were obliterated, and no Jews were permitted to pray at the site of the ancient Temple.

Peace has, at long last, been restored to the City of Peace. (The Hebrew name "Jerusalem" means "city of peace.") Confirming the new freedom for people of all faiths, the Patriarch of the Ethiopian Orthodox Church, the Greek Orthodox Patriarch, the National Council of American Nuns, and Mosel Kadi (Judge) Sheikh Toufik Assliya of Jaffa, have each paid tribute to Israel's hospitality to all religious groups.

In this newfound freedom, for the first time, archeologists from various parts of the world are presently engaged in uncovering the history of Jerusalem's past and revealing some of its ancient glories: Christian, Moslem and Jewish. They have given meaning to Isaiah's prophecy:

"For behold, I create new heavens and new earth . . .
Behold I create Jerusalem a rejoicing . . .
And it shall come to pass that
The wolf and the lamb shall feed together . . .
They shall not hurt nor destroy
In all My Holy mountain,"
Saith the Lord."

Is It Accurate to Speak
of *Jewish* Music, *Jewish* Art?

IT WOULD be correct to speak of certain types of music as
Jewish. The *traditional* chants, associated with synagogue
worship, are clearly Jewish. The distinctive melodies, associated
with the Reading of the Bible—properly termed, cantillation—
are authentically Jewish. A problem arises with regard to the
authenticity of the chanting of *prayers*. The worship heard in
a Bagdad synagogue bears no resemblance to that of an Eastern
European cantor. In the former case, the sounds are distinctly
Oriental; in the latter, one hears overtones of Slavic musical
modes.

The late Rabbi Abba Hillel Silver once referred satirically
to a custom that had been "hallowed by *twenty* years of tradition." One can regard much of modern folk music sung by
Jews at weddings and other happy occasions as being Jewish,
despite their borrowings from the folk music of Rumania,
Hungary and Russia. Jews have enjoyed this music for at least
a century.

Music written by Jews is certainly not necessarily Jewish.

But composers like Leonard Bernstein and Ernest Bloch have written music with Jewish themes. The test is ultimately whether such music contains a *Jewish* quality, that is, whether it is associated with the historic traditions of the people.

What has been said about music applies equally to art. A Jewish artist, depicting a New Testament theme, would not be producing Jewish art. Does that mean that the work of a non-Jewish artist, portraying an Old Testament character—Michelangelo's *David*—is Jewish art? Though I wept when I stood before the statue in Florence. I could not claim it as the art of my people. Since the personalities of the Hebrew Bible have been embraced by both Jews and Christians, it would be inaccurate to claim the Sistine Chapel scenes of the Garden of Eden and the Flood as Jewish.

Is There Such a Thing as Jewish Food?

OBVIOUSLY, we cannot point to any universal Jewish food. German Jews are unfamiliar with the folk dishes of their Eastern European brethren. Ethnic foods borrowed from their Slavic neighbors by Russian and Polish Jews may be regarded by many as Jewish, but a French or German Jew feels no sense of kinship with them. Generally, ethnic foods associated in the popular mind with various cultures are, in reality, the product of economic deprivation. Italian *pasta* was born out of poverty; so-called Irish dishes arose out of the needs of the poor; Jewish *gefilte* fish, stuffed fish, was the imaginative creation of the impoverished ghettoes of the Old World. Adding inexpensive bread or flour made it possible for a poor Jewish family to make a single fish serve a large number at the dinner table.

Two categories of food might be considered as authentically Jewish. One is, obviously, that which is dictated by Jewish ritual law: *matzoth*, the unleavened bread eaten on Passover; or kosher wine, prescribed for the Sabbath and festivals. A second consists of a variety of puddings called *kugel* and another similar delicacy called *cholent*, which grew out of Jewish religious law which forbade cooking or baking on the Sabbath. The ingenuity of the Jewish housewife enabled these Sabbath dishes to retain their warmth by judicious use of a low flame. Indubitably, one is safe in referring to a *kugel* or a *cholent* as Jewish food.

Some Recommended Books

In the course of my work I have frequently been asked to recommend "selected readings" on Jewish subjects. This is not too easily done—not if one is to be fair to the hundreds of worthwhile texts, essays, anthologies and works of fiction that have been written over the years on matters of Jewish interest. The selection of one book and the omission of another is entirely a matter of personal preference—and often bespeaks only a greater familiarity with certain volumes than with others.

These suggestions, therefore, are by no means to be considered as exhaustive of all the excellent material available. They do not include technical books used by specialists. They represent, like the rest of this book, an introduction which, I hope, will encourage broader reading and greater interest in this widely discussed area of literature.

RABBI MORRIS N. KERTZER

JEWISH LIFE IN THE MIDDLE AGES by Israel Abrahams, Edward Goldston, London.

    A delightful and warm description of family and community life in the Middle Ages.

ISRAEL, A PERSONAL HISTORY by David Ben-Gurion, Funk and Wagnalls.

A massive but lively book reflecting the thoughts of the architect of the Jewish state.

WHAT THE JEWS BELIEVE by Philip S. Bernstein, Farrar, Straus & Young, Inc.

A superb study of the Jewish outlook as revealed in its festivals.

THE WISDOM OF ISRAEL by Louis Browne, Randon House.

A careful collection of the literature of Israel from the Bible to modern times.

TALES OF THE HASIDIM: EARLY MASTERS by Martin Buber, Schoken Books. Paperback Edition.

GREAT JEWISH BOOKS, edited by Samuel Caplan and Harold Ribalow, Horizon Press, Inc.

A selection of outstanding Jewish writing.

EVERYMAN'S TALMUD by Abraham Cohen, E. P. Dutton & Company, Inc.

A splendid introduction to the *Talmud*.

PATHWAYS THROUGH THE BIBLE by Mortimer Cohen, Jewish Publication Society of America.

An excellent selection of the outstanding Old Testament passages and a commentary with fine insights.

JUDAISM IN THEORY AND IN PRACTICE by Beryl D. Cohon, Bloch Publishing Company, Inc.

A simple and factual presentation of Jewish beliefs and customs by a Reform rabbi.

TO BE A JEW by Hayim H. Donin, Basic Books.

A useful guide to Jewish observance.

MY PEOPLE by Abba Eban, Behrman House, Random House.

A vision of the Jewish people from the pen of the world's most eloquent orator.

JEWISH CUSTOMS AND CEREMONIES by Ben Edidin, Hebrew Publishing Company.

JEWISH HOLIDAYS AND FESTIVALS by Ben Edidin, Hebrew Publishing Company.

Two volumes containing excellent illustrations of various symbols in Judaism, written for high school students.

WHAT WE MEAN BY RELIGION by Ira Eisenstein, Jewish Reconstructionist Foundation.

A study of Jewish ideals based on High Holy Days.

THE JEWISH WAY OF LIFE by Isidore Epstein, Edward Goldston, London.

The social ideals of Judaism presented by an English rabbi.

HEAR, YE SONS by Irving Fineman, Longmans, Green and Company, Inc.

The mood and spirit of Jewish family life are excellently conveyed in this warm novel.

BELIEFS AND PRACTICES OF JUDAISM by Louis Finkelstein, Devin-Adair Company.

An outline of the essential teachings of Judaism by one of the world's foremost Jewish scholars.

THE JEWS, edited by Louis Finkelstein, Harper and Brothers.

A series of scholarly studies on every aspect of Jewish life.

PASSOVER: ITS HISTORY AND TRADITIONS by Theodore Gaster, Henry Schuman, Inc.

A brilliant analysis of the history and meaning of the festival of freedom.

MAN'S BEST HOPE by Roland B. Gittelsohn, Random House.

A modern approach to Jewish values, using the insights of contemporary science.

A HISTORY OF THE JEWS by Solomon Grayzel, Jewish Publication Society of America.

A scholarly work which tells the history of the Jews from the time of the destruction of the first Temple until the creation of the modern State of Israel.

LIFE IS WITH PEOPLE by Elizabeth Herzog and Mark Zborowski, International Universities Press, Inc.

A very readable description of the traditions and customs of small-town life among the Jews of Eastern Europe.

THE EARTH IS THE LORD'S by Abraham J. Heschel, Henry Schuman, Inc.

A small volume, beautifully written, portraying the religious and cultural life of Eastern European Jewry.

JEWISH VALUES by Louis Jacobs, Valentine-Mitchell.

A study of eleven basic Jewish ethical principles.

ISRAEL: A HISTORY OF THE JEWISH PEOPLE by Rufus Learsi, The World Publishing Company.

A well-written study that contains excellent chapters on the Jews in the modern world.

RABBINIC ANTHOLOGY by C. G. Montefiore and H. Loewe, Macmillan, London.

The most comprehensive selection of the sayings of the rabbis, with a particularly able analysis of Jewish-Christian relations.

HASIDIC ANTHOLOGY by Louis I. Newman and Samuel Spitz, Bloch Publishing Company, Inc.

An extensive collection of sayings of the Hasidic rabbis.

A HISTORY OF THE JEWS by Abram L. Sachar, Alfred A. Knopf, Inc.

An extremely readable one-volume work with special emphasis on the social approach.

THE COURSE OF MODERN JEWISH HISTORY by Howard Sachar, Dell Publishing.

The most comprehensive analysis of the twentieth-century Jews.

THE WORLD OF SHOLOM ALEICHEM by Maurice Samuel, Alfred A. Knopf, Inc.

An insight into the life and times of the Jewish Mark Twain.

THE JEWISH CARAVAN by Leo Schwartz, Rinehart & Company. The best anthology covering the entire sweep of Jewish literature.

THE JEWISH FESTIVALS by Hayyim Schauss, Union of American Hebrew Congregations.

THE LIFETIME OF A JEW by Hayyim Schauss, Union of American Hebrew Congregations.

BASIC JUDAISM by Milton Steinberg, Harcourt, Brace & Company.

A concise primer with information about the fundamental teachings of the Jewish faith—the best of its kind.

AS A DRIVEN LEAF by Milton Steinberg, The Bobbs-Merrill Company.

A superbly written story of talmudic times.

THE JEWS OF SILENCE by Elie Wiesel, Holt, Rinehart and Winston.

A moving portrayal of the plight of Soviet Jewry.

THE HOLY SCRIPTURES, published by the Jewish Publication Society of America.

This is the standard English translation of the Old Testament used by Jews.

Index

247